Comm

Demo

DATE DUE

The Library Store #47-0107

Maywood Public Library
121 S. 5th Ave.
Maywood, IL 60153

Common Sense Democracy

How to Complete the American Revolution in Your Neighborhood

Clayton Daughenbaugh

Copyright © 2003 by Clayton Daughenbaugh.

Library of Congress Number: 2003090630
ISBN : Softcover 1-4010-9469-4

All rights reserved. No part of this book may be reproduced or transmitted in any form or by any means, electronic or mechanical, including photocopying, recording, or by any information storage and retrieval system, without permission in writing from the copyright owner.

This book was printed in the United States of America.

To order additional copies of this book, contact:
Xlibris Corporation
1-888-795-4274
www.Xlibris.com
Orders@Xlibris.com
17952

Contents

ACKNOWLEDGMENT 9
INTRODUCTION 13
MISSIONARIES FOR DEMOCRACY 15
THE CONSTITUTIONAL VOID 21
CREATING PARALLEL GOVERNMENT 27
THE PEOPLE'S POWER 39
LAYING THE FOUNDATION FOR GAINING LOCAL DEMOCRATIC POWER 45
THE RITUALS OF DEMOCRACY 49
FROM RITUAL TO ORGANIZATION 64
RELUCTANT LEADERS 78
HONORABLE CITIZENS: THE PREREQUISITE FOR DEMOCRACY 82
PROFESSIONAL ORGANIZERS 88
"LAWS OF NATURE AND OF NATURE'S GOD" 91
AFTERWARD 95
APPENDIX ONE: THE SAVE OUR CITY COALITION PRINCIPLES AND PHILOSOPHY OF LOCAL DEMOCRATIC ORGANIZING 99

APPENDIX TWO:
VOLUNTEER LEADERSHIP 103
APPENDIX THREE: STRUCTURE AND DYNAMICS
OF A COMMUNITY ORGANIZATION 105
APPENDIX FOUR:
DEVELOPING A STRATEGIC
PLAN FOR WINNING AN ISSUE 111
APPENDIX FIVE: AN ORGANIZER'S JOB 113
APPENDIX SIX: AMENDING DEMOCRACY
INTO THE CONSTITUTION 116
APPENDIX SEVEN: EXCERPTS FROM
THOMAS JEFFERSON'S LETTERS
DESCRIBING THE 'WARD-REPUBLIC' 118
BIBLIOGRAPHY 123
ENDNOTES 125

DEDICATION

TO MY FAMILY:
LISA, LUKE, AND SAM DAUGHENBAUGH
AND
HOWARD AND JUDY DAUGHENBAUGH,
CINDY PERKINS, KAREN STRUNK

ACKNOWLEDGMENT

This book was written to communicate the model of organizing for local democracy practiced by the **Save Our City Coalition** (SOCC) and to encourage and support individuals interested in it. It would not be what it is without the participation of innumerable volunteers and staff over many years.

The final draft owes an immense debt to the editorial skills and intellect of Kimberly VanWagner. Carl Green and Patrick Murphy's review was important to the early drafts. Lisa Daughenbaugh, Judy & Howard Daughenbaugh and Roger Hartmann were helpful as the book progressed.

All the errors and oversights are, of course, my own.

If married, no career in organizing is possible without a very tolerant and supportive wife — Lisa has been outstanding.

"In the following pages I offer nothing more than simple facts, plain arguments, and common sense."

—"Common Sense", Thomas Paine, 1775.

"When in the course of human events it becomes necessary for one people to dissolve the political bands which have connected them with another, and to assume among the powers of the earth the separate and equal station to which the laws of nature and of nature's God entitle them, a decent respect to the opinions of mankind requires that they should declare the causes which impel them to the separation.

"We hold these truths to be self-evident: that all men are created equal; that they are endowed by their creator with certain inalienable rights; that among these are life, liberty, and the pursuit of happiness; that to secure these rights, governments are instituted among men, deriving their just powers from the consent of the governed; that whenever any form of government becomes destructive of these ends, it is the right of the people to alter or to abolish it, and to institute new government, laying out its foundations on such principles, and organizing it's powers in such form as to them shall seem most likely to effect their safety and happiness."

—Declaration of Independence, Thomas Jefferson, 1776.

"Liberty [is] power held by the people."

—"The Creation of the American Republic", Gordon Wood, p. 23.

INTRODUCTION

Common Sense Democracy is a patriot's guide to retaking control of America's political system. It identifies the power held by run-of-the-mill, every day, citizens and explains how and why it works. The book illustrates how, beginning on your own street, the people can accumulate the power necessary to call the shots in your community. It is a guide to the lost art of popular sovereignty.

From this book you will gain clarity regarding the muddled definition of democracy. America has laid claim to it, but our government is a republic, not a democracy. The difference is critical to the average citizens' ability to get things done in our communities. In our Constitution there is a great void where democracy ought to be. If we're going to have democracy in America there will need to be new institutions paralleling the existing republican ones and we'll have to make them ourselves.

You will also learn what constitutes a local democratic institution paralleling our republican government. If the people are to rule we must be organized to do so effectively. We must establish political structures enabling our communities to identify and execute policies. America doesn't need a new revolution to replace our government. We need to complete the one we started over two centuries ago.

Common Sense Democracy will describe the way in which power works from the bottom up. Although you may feel as though you have no input, power begins with you. The book will go through the steps you can take on your block, along with your neighbors, to create democracy on your street. It will explain how you can grow from a few small groups on several blocks to an organization empowering your entire community. You'll learn the qualities of leadership necessary to a properly functioning democratic organization and what professional skills you'll need from staff to support your organization.

Common Sense Democracy provides clear and practical guidance grounded in a solid analysis of how power works. Designed for contemporary political circumstances it does not neglect the lessons of history. Part manual and part manifesto it is concise—a quick read for 21st Century patriots. Do what this book suggests and you can help your community determine its own destiny.

—Clayton Daughenbaugh

MISSIONARIES FOR DEMOCRACY

If we're to believe the newspapers, democracy means "free and fair" elections.

"Free and fair" elections do not constitute democracy. They create a republic. A republic is when the People select an "elite" segment of the population to govern society during the time between elections.

Democracy occurs when the people govern society directly. Majority rule is the core principle of democracy. The rulers, if any such power is delegated, are generally kept on a tight leash and subject to short terms of office and frequent rotation (i.e. term limits).

When was the last time you, together with your fellows, had a direct personal hand in the governing of your country, of your city, or even of your neighborhood?

America is largely a liberal republic. The liberal tradition, primarily a gift from Britain, holds that there are basic rights that no one, not kings nor republics nor democracies, can take from individuals.

Thus the creation of the Bill of Rights and the tradition of minority rights within majority rule. In a pure republican tradition, the elected "elite" governs via selfless service to the public interest.[1] This noble concept is one the founding fathers thought a bit too optimistic, deciding instead that America's republic should function in accordance with the Madisonian principle of a "balance of powers" in which the people's power is factionalized by, and pitted against, a distant centralized government that is itself divided into three separate branches.

The balance of powers has become unbalanced. The vigorous assertion of popular governance to which the Constitution was the designed counterweight[2] may soon need to be placed on the political endangered species list. The elites have gained too much influence at the expense of the people. There is too little democracy in the mix of America's governing institutions. In fact, democracy has no formal place within the framework of the nation's political institutions.

To the eternal discredit of America's founding fathers, there is no provision for democracy in the Constitution. There are detailed provisions for the functioning of a republic. The Bill of Rights guarantees each American essential individual rights. But nowhere in the Constitution is there any mention of the people coming together to make decisions determining how society will function. The faith of the people in their sovereignty, combined with the freedoms that are in fact guaranteed in the Constitution, has kept the light of liberty shining through the nation's history. But in the last quarter of the 20th Century that light has been reduced to a flicker.

Thomas Jefferson identified this void in our Constitution in the latter years of his life as he reflected on what the founders had accomplished. After noting that the most desirable means of government is "government by its citizens in mass, acting directly and personally," he says "[I]t must be agreed our governments have much less . . . than ought to have been expected."[3]

In an earlier letter Jefferson had proposed his solution—the creation of local ward-republics—based on his observation that democracy is particularly suited to very local government. He saw this solution as so critical to "the control of the people over the organs of their government"[4] that the entire constitutional framework for America's government should be built upon it:

> "The elementary republics of the wards, the county republics, the State republics, and the republic of the Union, would form a gradation of authorities, standing each on the basis of law, holding every one its delegated share of powers, and constituting truly a system of fundamental balances and checks for the government. Where every man is a sharer in the direction of his ward—republic, or of some of the higher ones, and feels that he is a participator in the government of affairs, not merely at an election one day in the year but every day; when there shall not be a man in the State who will not be a member of some one of its councils, great or small . . ."[5]

Jefferson, clearly aware there was no place for the people to balance the powers, feared that an aristocratic elite would supplant the sovereignty of the people within the new American republic. The ward-republics were his proposed solution to this crucial void.[6]

Jefferson's fears are coming true.

A pervasive sense of powerlessness is found among the people in both reduced participation in citizen-based efforts to address everyday problems and the lack of street-level democracy whereby citizens enforce the informal social mores which solidify the bonds of community. The lack of strong, effective democratic institutions has left the people inexperienced and seemingly powerless in the face of modern bureaucracy, technology, and capital conglomerates (be they corporate or government). There is a crying need for an effective means of direct citizen participation in the general governing of our society.

Americans are delegating the responsibility for society upstairs to the corporate and governmental elite. "You can't fight City Hall" has become an article of faith. People believe they can no longer be effective and are withdrawing from public life. That act of withdrawal is a free gift of power to the elite that stands ready and willing to exercise it.

Democracy is more than a system of government. It is the participation of people, based on the ideal of equality, in all areas of public life. The relationships which grow from this common enterprise are the foundation for the nation's civic life—they bind us together as a people. Since we lack an institutional framework for active democracy participation in civic life is reduced and the ties that bind America together are disintegrating. Corresponding to the fall of democracy has been a rise in the prominence of hierarchical institutions. The combination of modern bureaucracy, technology, and consolidated capital has removed many of the public decisions effecting day-to-day life from the local level. They have become decisions made by distant elites—only some of whom are elected. Without an institutionalized balance of power at the local level, people will lack the means to assert the authority that is rightfully theirs.

The lack of democratic institutions not only leaves people without the means to assert their authority, it also leaves them ignorant of how to do so. Such ignorance reduces people's ability to extract resources from local government and has a profound impact on the day-to-day interactions in which people regulate the quality of their community life.

The importance of citizen empowerment to the quality of local life has been documented by the current "Project on Human Development" being conducted in Chicago by the Harvard School of Public Health. Tying "collective efficacy" to levels of street crime, a recent *Science* magazine article drawing on this study noted:

> "The capacity of residents to control group level processes and visible signs of social disorder is thus a key mechanism influencing opportunities for interpersonal crime in a neighborhood. Informal social control also generalizes to broader issues of import to the

> well-being of neighborhoods. In particular, the differential ability of communities to extract resources and respond to cuts in public services (such as police patrols, fire stations, garbage collection, and housing code enforcement) looms large . . ."[7]

This is scientific evidence that the collective power to achieve results has a profound impact on local community life. Without such power, people will have less ability to reduce crime or to secure governmental support for our neighborhoods. Without an institutional framework for democracy at the local level our increasingly transient and multi-cultural society will not have the knowledge, skill, or the means to maintain healthy communities.

Some would point to the proliferation of citizen-based interest groups in society as a counter to the thesis that local democracy is wanting. However, these organizations are largely based on a select group of institutional leaders who speak on behalf of a large number of constituents. Such organizations do not get down to the street level of our neighborhoods and thus only partially address the lack of democracy in America. This lack of street-level democracy results in an inability of citizens to have a positive influence on the problems of modern life at the local level.[8] Groups acting on behalf of others are no substitute for people acting together in their own common interest.

If a slow death of America's liberty is to be prevented, Americans must become missionaries for democracy. The mission is to empower citizens at the most local of levels—to fill the constitutional void, identified by Jefferson, that undermines the democratic foundations of the American revolution.

The 21st Century Patriot must create and support local organizations of parallel government. These organizations are democratically built, basing their actions on the documented support of the majority of affected citizens for the supported position, with forums for the development of organizational positions where all residents are entitled to speak and vote. Their strength must be derived from the organized force of average citizens participating directly in the governing of their community. A democratic organization recognizes that power is not derived from ties to political, bureaucratic, or economic "elites".

Such an organization also knows that democratic power cannot be exercised by representatives who do not actively consult and obtain approval from the people prior to staking out organizational positions on community concerns.

The 21st Century Patriot should head for the backstreets and the country roads. If you want to breathe life into America's democracy, you can't do it from the halls of Congress, the lawns of academia, the local courthouse, or the privacy of a charitable storefront. Democracy lives on our streets and in our homes. It breathes wherever people come together to identify and support a common cause, not of an ideological or cultural segment of society, but of the combined masses who today form the passive and silent majority.

Democracy is not a handful of isolated protesters blocking traffic two miles from the Democratic or Republican convention. Democracy is citizens meeting together to identify common concerns, going door-to-door enlisting support for proposed solutions, and then going directly to the elected or corporate elite to tell them what to do. Democracy is not government giving out free cheese to help the poor. Democracy is citizens together demanding their government provide tools and seeds so they can grow their own food. Democracy is not a government regulated monopoly putting us all on some sputtering corporate power grid. Democracy is citizens picking and choosing from a multiplicity of power sources and creating some new ones of their own. Democracy is not an election every two or four years. Democracy is government by the people, in mass, acting directly and personally.

THE CONSTITUTIONAL VOID

The United States Constitution establishes a Republic, not a democracy. All official power is exercised by elected representatives and their appointees. This establishment is made very explicit in Article IV, Section 4 which states, "The United States shall guarantee to every State in this Union a Republican Form of Government . . ."

Nowhere does the Constitution provide for the direct governance of any portion of society by the People themselves. The closest it comes is the First Amendment: "Congress shall make no law . . . abridging the freedom of speech, or of the press, or the right of the people peaceably to assemble, and to petition the Government for redress of grievances". While the rights to assemble and petition allow people to form associations to pressure the established authorities, there is no provision for direct governance by the people. Without an institutionalized presence, the people must repeatedly reinvent democratic organization while the republic is granted a permanent organizational head start.

The extent to which people should govern society directly has been at issue since the founding of America. While the heritage of the Declaration of Independence and community-reliance has kept the spirit of democracy alive, the lack of a

Constitutional article establishing a framework means democracy's implementation remains an uphill struggle.

Approval of the Constitution was very controversial in its day. The "antifederalists" put up a vigorous opposition. The distancing of power from the people was, as explained by Gordon Wood, the key underlying issue:

> "The Antifederalists thus came to oppose the new national government for the same reason the Federalists favored it: because its very structure and detachment from the people would work to exclude any kind of actual and local interest representation and prevent those who were not rich, well born, or prominent from exercising political power. Both sides fully appreciated the central issue the Constitution posed and grappled with it throughout the debates: whether a professedly popular government should actually be in the hands of, rather than simply derived from, common ordinary people."[9]

Neither party, however, proposed any genuinely democratic means of government and, in the end, the 'federalist' vision predominated.

The original Constitution provided for direct election only of the House of Representatives. The President was (and still is) elected by "electors" chosen by each state. The Senate was appointed by the legislatures of each state. The definition of the right to vote was left to each individual state, generally being restricted to property holding white males. The right to vote itself was only relevant to one half of one of the three branches of the federal government. America, despite the great leap forward in liberty it represented, barely qualified as a republic under the original terms of its own Constitution.

The trend over the years has been towards an increase in the formal sovereignty of the people within the Constitution: the 'Bill of Rights' (included in order to overcome the 'anti-federalist' opposition) was the first step; the abolition of slavery in the 13th

Amendment and the granting of citizenship rights to all born or naturalized in the United States by the 14th Amendment greatly expanded the definition of "the people"; the passage of the 15th Amendment in 1870 extended the right to vote to all males; in 1913 the People were finally granted full authority to elect the Senate by the 27th Amendment; women gained the right to vote in 1920; a two term limit was placed on the presidency in 1951; poll taxes were eliminated in 1964; eighteen through twenty-one year olds were granted the vote in 1971. It is an impressive record of progress, but it still does not contain any provision for direct governance by the People.

Thomas Jefferson's proposal for ward-republics would have filled this void had it been incorporated into the Constitution. The ward-republics, by providing a forum for people to gather together to make decisions, recognized the essential aspect of formal discussion, in addition to voting, in the democratic process. If the people are to effectively exercise power, they must not allow themselves to be reduced to atomized individuals voting in private booths.

The availability of citizen-initiated referenda in some states goes a long way towards democratizing the political process. However, a referenda process does not provide for people coming together for the sole reason of exercising their democratic power—it provides for no organization other than what is necessary to address a single issue. This is sporadic democracy, effective only on single issues and only on election day. The people are still required to rebuild democratic organizational structures each time a new issue comes along. With the permanent head start granted by the Constitution, the republic enjoys a sizable advantage over any upstart democratic organization that may seek to challenge the republican reign.

The 'ward republics' would equal the playing field by enabling the People to gather, deliberate, and decide in between elections on whatever issues are deemed significant. They would provide an essential element of regular and frequent accountability of the government to the people that is lacking in the institutional framework provided by the Constitution. The people could exercise their sovereignty without having to overcome the republic's organizational head start.

Amending the Constitution would require a national movement on behalf of democracy, something akin to the populist movement of the late 19th Century which sought to redraw the American political landscape.

The "Farmer's Alliance," founded on a small farm in Lampasas County, Texas in September of 1877, ultimately grew into a large multi-state organization covering two-thirds of the nation that metamorphosed into the People's Party.[10] The Alliance had a solid grassroots base built on local county organizations. Its leaders were indigenous to its constituency. It spread via lecturers (organizers) sent out on the road recruiting people to join its cooperative. It was a self-funded organization with its own independent press and involved the broad masses of people including, unique for its day, southern black farmers. The Alliance duplicated its county structure across Texas, the South, and much of the Great Plains. At its height it made inroads into the West and Midwest. For one brief moment, until it was co-opted by William Jennings Bryan and the modern Democratic Party, the Populists were challenging and on the verge of supplanting the elitist political apparatus that dominates America to this day.

If there is ever to be a mass democratic movement to reform America's political institutions, it will likely have to follow the Alliance model: a federation of local organizations run by indigenous leadership with financial independence sufficient to hire its own staff and maintain its own communications infrastructure, all of which is sufficiently integrated to provide a power structure flowing from the bottom up.

America's democratic tradition of majority rule is losing the competition with its republican counterpart. Democracy is losing because there is no vehicle by which the common interest can be made incarnate in the nation's political life. The democratic fire that gave birth to the American nation has gone from flame to flicker.

The fire of liberty burned hot in the middle of the 18th Century when Americans first applied the concept of parallel government via the Continental Congress. It was the place where the patriots of 1776 organized the intercolonial resistance to British tyranny. All sorts of local committees and councils were established to carry on the quasi-governmental work of the Congress. In some cases, with British failure to recognize the sovereignty of the people going to greater and greater extremes, the colonial legislatures themselves became organs of the parallel government.[11] American democracy was born in these grassroots organizations and matured into a nation when the British empire refused to respect the democratic reality and the People, more via resistance and non-compliance than with guns, overthrew the colonial tyranny.[12]

During the Great Depression the greatest organizational expression of democracy was the creation of the Congress of Industrial Unions (CIO).

The CIO was the first mass-based union organizing drive. Organizing across all lines of ethnicity and skills, it strove to represent not just the members of its unions, but workers across the nation.[13]

The victories of the CIO enabled A. Philip Randolph to complete the organization of the sleeping car porters and move on to the first mass based protests by African-Americans. That heritage was transferred to sympathetic ears at the Southern Christian Leadership Conference, where the practice of applying majority-based organizing to local communities was put to work as the civil rights movement spread across the country.[14]

The empowerment of neighborhoods made a huge step forward when Saul Alinsky, also greatly influenced by CIO organizing, devised the first form of parallel government at the local level.[15] Alinsky's emphasis on native leadership and an organizational structure built around residency in a defined community area was the genesis of the modern community organization.

The combination of these two approaches to organizing local

communities—an invitation to participation for, and representation of, the majority of citizens along with a formal legislative structure for the community—can give rise to truly democratic forms of parallel government at the local level. Here is new life for Jefferson's ward-republics and oxygen for the flickering flame of American democracy.

CREATING PARALLEL GOVERNMENT

"An association simply consists in the public and formal support of specific doctrines by a certain number of individuals who have undertaken to cooperate in a stated way in order to make these doctrines prevail . . . they form something like a separate nation within the nation and a government within the government."[16]

Given the Constitutional void of democratic institutions, the people alone possess the power to create them. The role of such democratic organizations is to parallel, not replace, the republican government. They provide the means by which the people can establish their own priorities, independent of the structures of the republic, and work to see them implemented. Parallel democratic structures can accomplish their ends either via engaging republican structures directly or by circumventing them entirely. To be effective these institutions must have both legislative and executive arms to identify and affect the will of the people. To be successful democratic associations must be founded on certain core principles and their institutional arms must follow several essential processes.

A democratic organization must be:

— majority-based, with guarantees for minority rights
— independent of election-based organizations (political parties)
— seeking routine accountability of governmental and corporate institutions to the People year round.

What is "majority-based"? It is the process of constant outreach to the community for input and ratification. It is a process that places people before issues. A "majority-based" organization places the process of citizen involvement and empowerment at the center of its organizational identity—all must have an equal opportunity for voice and vote. The issues will come and go. The process will remain constant.

A majority-based organization seeks to represent a cross-section of the entire community which it serves. It is not built around a certain segment of society such as church members or ethnic groups unless those groups form an overwhelming majority of the community's citizens.

A majority-based organization can be contrasted to an "issue organization" (more commonly known as a special interest group). In an issue organization, participants are determined by who supports the stated issue of the organization. For instance, the purpose of the Sierra Club is "To explore, enjoy, and protect the wild places of the earth . . ."[17] Participants in the Sierra Club support that concept. People who do not will choose to be part of some other special interest.

A majority-based organization will be a multi-issue organization. The issues will, most likely, not be tied together by any particular theme such as environment, economic development, or housing. Those participating in efforts involving one issue may not even agree with the organization's position on another issue.

The central purpose of a majority-based organization is

democracy—the direct involvement of a majority of individuals in specific aspects of the governing of society. You are a member of a "majority-based" organization in the same way that you are a citizen of the country—you live within its defined territory.

Why should such an organization remain **independent of partisan organizations?** Partisan political organizations are focused on getting power from people and granting it to particular individuals and thus they are republican in character. Democratic organizations are focused on retaining power for, and dispersing the authority to exercise it among, the people. Indeed, it is the people themselves who constitute the organization.

In a partisan organization, the people's concerns are addressed via the authority granted to the organization's leaders. You go to the alderman or congressman or president (or her assigned subordinates) and ask for a favor. The favor is generally granted depending on your readiness to participate in the effort to maintain or advance the elected position of the leader. The principle is the same whether it is individuals seeking a trash can or Political Action Committees seeking a regulatory ruling. If you don't support the official or the 'party' you're not likely to get your trash can or your regulation. The closer your ties to the partisan organization the more dependent you are on it.

In a majority-based organization, people's concerns are addressed via the authority of the people organized. If the alderman or congressman or president wants a favorable review from the people on the particular concern when they go to vote, he will do what the organization wants. If the official opposes too many of those concerns, the people's performance review may be negative and they may chose to remove the grant of authority they have given to the leader and give it to someone else.

It is, of course, entirely possible that a People's organization and a partisan organization can have a cooperative relationship—assuming that relationship is based upon mutual respect for the integrity of each other. However, if a partisan organization fails to respect the role of a democratic one, conflict will be essential if respect is to be gained.

Democratic organizations should **seek routine accountability of governmental and corporate institutions year round.** The principled reason, as eloquently expressed in the Declaration of Independence, is that in our society the people are sovereign. Although governments and corporations have profound impacts on local communities, their interests are not identical with those communities.

The practical reason is that there are multiplying organizational levels that act as barriers between these institutions and the people living in the places they impact. The institutional decision makers are often not even aware of, and maybe not interested in, the circumstances in the communities on which they are impacting. Just calling a governmental or corporate bureaucracy on the phone can be a trying experience. Actually engaging a decision maker in a discussion about the impacts of his decisions on your community is virtually impossible—unless your community is organized to force the issue.

The founders, deliberately established a distance between republican government and its people. James Madison, in order to avoid the tyranny of the majority, took all democratic options, except for the vote, away from the people.[18] While his method accomplished its goal, it left the people with no constitutionally guaranteed means of governing themselves and therefore left them at the mercy of the elected elite which itself is subject to the appeal of minority factions ("special interests") in opposition to the majority interest. His response to this problem was, "If a faction consists of less than a majority, relief is supplied by the republican principle, which enables the majority to defeat its sinister views by regular vote." This, unfortunately, fails to take into account that the Republic will act every day of the year yet elections are held, at most, only one day every two years. The majority is left formally impotent except on the one day of elections. While the tyranny of the majority is prevented in

Madison's republican scheme, the majority is left with no mechanism to defend itself. By making no provision for a democracy to parallel the republic, Madison left the majority no means of organizing to counter the multiple daily tyrannies of multiple minority interests. The "special interests" govern while the common interest is silenced.[19]

In Madison's scheme, the purpose of the elected elite is both to represent the people and to buffer the government from the people. The large hired and appointed bureaucracy that actually carries out the necessary functions of government also serves to increase this distance. Government employees will typically see themselves as accountable first to those doing the hiring rather than to the people who provide the funds for their salaries.

There is a natural tension between the people and their government.

However, when the people are not organized to exercise their rights and responsibilities they, in effect, avoid the tension by habitually and ignorantly surrendering their consent to the governing elite. Their own inaction leads to the benign oppression of the welfare state. The solution to this dilemma is a democratic government paired with and parallel to the republican. Madison wasn't so much wrong as he was incomplete. By creating parallel institutions, which they directly control, the people exercise their god-given ability to grant and withdraw consent.

Corporations are even more distant than government, as their structure allows an even greater buffer between their policies and the will of the people. With a corporation, no one is elected by the general public and, therefore, there is no one to whom the people can turn to readily leverage accountability of the corporation to local communities. The original concept of the people's government granting corporate charters allowing private interests to conduct business that benefits the public has been lost. Rarely do you see government revoke a corporation's charter as a consequence of activities inimical to the public interest. What was once a privilege, to conduct government granted business, has become a virtual right.

The forfeiture of the revocation tool has left corporations accountable to few organized entities outside of their own stockholders and the government's plethora of regulatory bureaucrats. There is little practical accountability to the people's elected representatives and no institutional structure for the people themselves to hold these entities directly accountable for their actions.

The People organized can have an impact on corporate policy, but it is a struggle. Corporate accountability to local communities can only be affected by independent democratic organizations.

So how is a democratic organization's parallel government structured? How does it work? The structure is divided into two categories: legislative and executive.

LEGISLATIVE

The legislative realm is the core of any democratic organization as it is the locale of decisions regarding the community. In a democratic organization the legislature is not elected because the people decide and act directly. It is open to all who reside within the bounds of the organization. Therefore, the decision making process must have provision for incorporating the maximum number of community residents as possible.

The legislative process has a pair of goals: defining and winning issues. An issue is a tangible and resolvable (i.e. winnable) concern, felt by a majority of the people in a definable population, which they are willing to commit time and energy to resolving.

To define and win community issues the legislative process must include five elements: listening, composing, proposing, deciding, and implementing. While there is a general progression in time of one to the other you must keep in mind that the relationship of these elements is organic, not mechanical. Each element contains portions of the other, they grow together to create the whole.

Listening is the crucial first stage to identifying the people's needs and concerns. At the first level, it's very informal. As you go about your normal day-to-day business, people talk, you listen. When many people bring up the same concern you need to listen carefully for clues to the underlying reasons for the importance of the concern. Make a plan to speak with residents, identify how the individual concerns are linked to form a larger community concern and assess whether the concern may be sufficient to become an issue.

Composing is the next element. A committee meeting will need to be called to discuss the results of the listening process. This meeting should be open to all, with specific invitations sent to those who participated in it. Of course not all will come, but the principle of openness is critical to maintaining a truly democratic process. This discussion will result in written language for the prospective issue.

At this point it's time for *proposing* the issue to the community.

Call a community meeting. It will have three purposes: to fully explain the issue, to gain an authorization vote for putting it before the community, and to line up the volunteers necessary to solicit and collect signatures from the community in favor of the issue.

Now its time to *decide*. This is the step that corresponds to the typical legislative action of voting on a bill. The volunteers are going door-to-door explaining the issue to their neighbors and asking them to sign their support. If there is an advisory or binding referenda process available, this signature collection step can become the petition for getting your issue on the ballot for an actual vote. Either way, this is the critical moment of assembling the consents of the residents. People are informed and, based on the information provided, they decide. You now have the three elements of an issue: a tangible concern which is demonstrably shared by a majority of the people that they have committed time and energy to resolving.

Once the issue has been decided, it's time for *implementation*. Unlike in typical government structures, this is also a legislative step. It should involve open "implementation committee" meetings where the deliberations necessary to carry on a campaign for the issue are conducted. There will be information to disperse and action proposals to plan. All the people impacted should have the opportunity for a voice and a vote at these meetings. In addition, it is critical that there be an ongoing public education portion of the campaign (flyers, mailings, newsletters, free-media, etc.) so that the general population is kept informed, regardless of attendance at the meetings. A successful majority-based issue campaign will also give appropriate opportunities for participation (phone blitzes, more signatures, special actions, etc.) to all residents. Having gained the support of the majority, you want to maintain the authority you've been granted by respecting the people's right to continue to make an informed decision on behalf of the issue. In a democratic system people can and will reconsider their grant of consent at any time.

If you don't respect this truth you're likely to lose their consent.

In a republican legislative structure, the representatives follow a similar process: they listen to their constituents, write and introduce a bill, the bill goes through a committee process, and it is finally debated and voted on by the entire legislative body. The striking difference in the democratic parallel is that there are no elected representatives deciding. In every case, it's the people themselves who must do so. The power to decide is kept in the hands of the people by having the implementation of the decision kept open to broad participation.

EXECUTIVE

Granting of all decision making and most implementation regarding community issues to the legislative "branch" of a democratic organization leaves less for the executive than is usual in a republican system. That is, of course, exactly the point. The power resides in the people.

An individual stripped of virtually all legislative functions is the first distinguishing factor of a democratic executive. The second is that the democratic executive is not an individual, but a collective, composed of volunteer leaders with the close assistance of staff. The lack of a single office holder disperses this critical authority and reinforces the concept of the dispersion of power among the people.

The Executive in a democratic organization has two primary functions. The first is the typical fiduciary responsibility of any board of directors—providing infrastructure for the organization (money, staff, office). The second is judicial in nature. The executive must insure the organization remains loyal to democratic principles and processes. The fiduciary responsibility is a particularly difficult one in this case because there are no easy sources of funds or staff for this type of organization. Fundraising is an essential task. Locating sources of funds that do not compromise the organization's independence is a very difficult. It certainly wouldn't do to depend on government grants. Getting your money from the very same institution that you must hold accountable to the people would dramatically limit your ability to do the job. You would not be able to tackle the hard issues.

A democratic organization will need to raise the majority of its funds itself. The executive will need to piece together a variety of means to gain money. How that is best done will vary from community to community. Charitable gaming (bingo, raffles) can be a good one. Large annual festivals might be another. Mail appeals or door-to-door canvases can help. "Community Service Directories" containing ads bought by local businesses are another traditional means. You can supplement these funds with a few grants, but you'll need to be financially independent in order to remain politically independent.

Private foundations are generally unlikely to provide funds for this type of organization.[20] They want to know what projects their money is impacting and that the work of the grantees will reflect favorably on the foundation among the influential people who provide the foundation with money or social standing. Typically this means they want to know what the issues will be so they can pass judgment. Since predicting, or worse yet predetermining, issues is antithetical to the central purpose of a democratic organization, the number of foundations even willing to consider such a proposal is limited. Add to this the definition of membership (simply residing in a particular area) and most foundations will not see a democratic organization as one in which they feel secure enough to give their money away. There are exceptions, but granting funds for the general purpose of empowering the broad masses is not fashionable in the foundation community.[21] Should you get a grant it will generally be only for a limited period of time (three years is a common maximum) and the foundation may change its priorities, thus suddenly shortening even further the time in which its funding might be available. The bottom line is that even if you can get foundation money it is rarely a reliable source of long term funding.

Whatever the combination of funding sources is, an institution of parallel government with sufficient staff to support its volunteer base must think in terms of tens or hundreds of thousands of dollars. That is hard work.

Finding good staff and training them are also very difficult tasks. Even those organizations that do "community organizing" often do not comport themselves by democratic principles. Therefore one cannot assume that hiring a professional organizer will automatically provide support for a majority-based organization. For example, the original Alinsky model of an "organization of organizations"[22] was built on a definition of leadership which emphasized their influence over followers. An organizer trained in that methodology might well bring many excellent attributes, but he would need special training to apply the principles of a democratic organization.[23] Simply hiring an organizer, no matter how great his experience might be, is not the answer. The executive must ensure, via its own direct oversight or by delegating it to a staff director, that the staff will not deviate from democratic principles and drift into a republican methodology.

This brings us to the second role of the Executive—the judicial practice of ensuring fidelity to democratic principles. When staff or volunteers fail to conform with the three core principles of a democratic organization (see the first page of this chapter) the executive must intervene and set matters straight.

A democratic organization must strive to base its decisions on the collected consents of the majority of the voting age individuals in the area that it represents. If elements of the organization attempt to shut out the voice of some segment of the community, that too must be stopped. If it is not stopped, the organization is a failure democratically, and should be dissolved or abandoned.

Republican organizations, while important and useful, do not fulfill the function of democratic organizations. Given the generally non-democratic structure of contemporary American society, democratic organizations must remain ever self-vigilant if they are to maintain their integrity.

Fidelity to democratic principles is essential if there is to be a truly democratic parallel to our republican institutions; however, fidelity is not sufficient. Effective democratic organizations must also have a clear conception of how democratic power works. That is the topic to which we will now turn.

THE PEOPLE'S POWER

"The people's power . . . is like the light of the sun, native, original, inherent, and unlimited by human authority. Power in the rulers . . . is like the reflected light of the moon, and is only borrowed, delegated and limited by the grant of the people."[24]

Power is the ability to get things done. Everyone has both the ability to think and work, and the ability to influence associates.

Political power is organization: the ability to gain, maintain, and direct collective consent.

Democratic power is political power exercised by a majority.

To gain democratic power it is essential to know how it works and how it relates to the governing of society. As Americans, we have a clear description of each in the Declaration of Independence:

"Governments are instituted among Men, deriving their just Powers from the Consent of the Governed . . . it is the right of the people to alter or to abolish it, and to institute new government, laying out its foundations on such principles, and organizing its powers in such form as to them shall seem most likely to effect their safety and happiness."

Power works from the bottom up. The people at the top, there only because the rest of us consent to it, are the most dependent people in the world. Their "throne" sits way up high on a power structure with many vital links made up of many integral parts. These links are groups of individuals. Weaken a link, and that structure sways. The people at the top must act to repair the damage or they might fall off in the swaying. Removing the obedience of a group means the rulers are ruling less. Keep chipping or hacking away at the links and the occupants of the throne must eliminate or accommodate the force that is eroding their power structure. The rulers, if they are to halt the erosion and maintain their position, must respond to the expanding group of people now exercising their independence. If the rulers fail and the people succeed, the structure will keep swaying and the occupants of the throne will fall off—some other group will get to sit on top of the existing structure.

If those on the "throne" hang on despite the swaying, the structure will become too top heavy and collapse. Those who cause the swaying will have the opportunity to pick up the pieces and put a whole new structure together.

Most of the pieces of a power structure are people. People aren't bricks and they don't always stay where put. Not only do they move about, they can decide on their own when they will move and to where. If people are to remain in their assigned position within the power structure, they must decide to do so—they must consent.

While moving about people also talk. That talk can lead to cooperation—a group of people acting together based on mutual consent. If a bunch of Peopleparts move at the same time, in the same direction, they could remove a link. Once organized they will have their own smaller political power structure.

When links move, a structure changes. If a majority of the Peopleparts move in unison, the power structure is transformed.

Something new will take place of the old. There will be a new throne—a throne which is built broadly and close to the base, where each part's participation in the structure is more equal. Such a throne is much less likely to sway or fall. That power structure is democracy.

In America's power structure, a republic, the top is a distance away from the base, the People. Nevertheless the occupants of the "throne" are close enough to the base that they remain aware of their dependency upon our consent. A republic has a fine tool to remind the occupants of the throne of their dependency upon the base—the election. Elections are a built in opportunity for people either to weaken or reinforce the power structure.

However, elections can also be a mask, hiding the ever-present opportunity to reduce or remove consent. Elections occur periodically for only one day, but power is exercised and consent is granted every day. If you want power you will not get it by focusing your attention on the republic's occasional day of reckoning. To obtain power you must act frequently.

To exercise power you must routinely gain, maintain, and direct consents. People are the source of consent. Consent is given one person at a time. Each individual must decide whether to grant someone else the authority to act on his behalf. When one person consents to allow another to direct his actions he then becomes obedient.

The motivations to grant another person authority can be placed into one of three categories:

— willing consent (given by active choice to obtain something good);
— apathetic consent (given by a failure to act);
— coerced consent (given by choice to avoid something bad).

Studying each will help you to gain consents and thus power.

Types of Willing Consent

This is the category of those who have been conscious of their choice to grant consent.

Trust is one of the best reasons to grant consent. When, over time, one person learns that another will act reliably in accordance with his values, he is very likely to agree to her requests. This is the essence of the leader/follower relationship.

Self-interest is another reason. A person is likely to grant authority if he perceives that he will gain a personal benefit from the act. This need not be limited to purely material gains. Prestige can often be a motivator. Gaining a share of the power may create loyalty and consent will thereby be granted over an extended time.

Common interest is often underrated as a reason for the granting of consent. Most people identify closely with their family, friends, community, lands, institutions, nationality, or country—all are common interests. Indeed, it is within these relationships that one gains happiness. In order to protect a common interest, individuals will sometimes make a sacrifice, offer a contribution, or do a little work.

Habit is the last, and most enduring, of the "voluntary" reasons for consent. An individual may have always done things a certain way and never thought about doing them differently.

Types of Apathetic Consent

This is the category of those who decide by not deciding. Their inactions will generally lend support to the existing power structure.

Ignorance is a common source of apathetic consent. Many people are simply unaware of what is at stake. Once informed, by a source they consider credible, they will often move into the category of willing consentors.

Disbelief, or lack of faith, in their own individual or collective ability to effect the outcome is the most difficult source of apathy to overcome. It generally results from an emotional limitation, a reasoned opinion, or some combination of the two. If these individuals are to move towards active consent they must be persuaded to suspend their judgment and grant some provisional authority.

Lack of interest is the final source of apathetic consent. Some people simply don't care. More common is an immediate, acute, or impending crisis in the lives of individuals which leaves them unable to care. Illness, mental or physical, is a frequent contributor.

Those who are apathetic due to ignorance or disbelief can be persuaded to change. Those suffering from lack of interest are generally a lost cause except in those rare circumstances when outside events affect them in the most directly personal of ways.

Types of Coerced Consent

Intimidation is the most common form of coercion. It is often imagined or brought about by implication. Just think of all the ways everyone is dependent upon the actions of other people. Is your local government official unhappy with something you've done or said? Do you need your trash picked up? Perhaps that official might suggest a delay in your trash pickup if you continue doing what he doesn't like. A little hint here, a bit of threat there, could well induce you to grant consent on one matter in order to avoid creating problems with another.

Falling victim to intimidation is generally avoidable. There typically are alternatives which could preclude the effectiveness of any manifestation of actual intimidation. Often simply "calling the bluff" will overcome the intimidating factor.

Fear is a response to a greater level of intimidation because the consequences are potentially more profound and perhaps unavoidable. You will lose something critical or precious if you refuse consent. A choice must be made. What among the things you most value do you value the greatest? There will be pain and harm either way.

Harassment is coercion through inconvenience. It is brought about by the regular disruption of otherwise normal or routine events. Its message is consent to 'A' if you want to continue enjoying 'B'. It is effective in coercing consent on matters of preference, as opposed to those of great value or necessity. If a union wants a raise they may win it via work slow downs, interruptions of daily routine, or public embarrassment. None of these would effect the employer's ability to remain in business though they will disrupt the normal conduct of his work.

All of these various categories and types of consent have one thing in common. They are based on the decisions of individuals. A person cannot be forced to consent.[25] However, we live in a dynamic world of consents given and withheld based upon perceptions of relative value. In order to live effectively in this world, you must consciously exercise your liberty—your ability to give and organize consent.

LAYING THE FOUNDATION FOR GAINING LOCAL DEMOCRATIC POWER

". . . of the people, by the people, for the people."

You gain power by combining consents. If power is going to be democratic it must have the consent of the majority. To effect democratic power, you must assemble the majority and defeat (through acquiescence, conversion, or coercion) the minority power structure.

Most republic-based power structures are "minority-based", inasmuch as they depend upon the 'willing consent' of a minority of the people and the 'apathetic consent' of enough other people to give them a majority of the consents.

A democratic power structure is "majority-based"—it has assembled the "willing consent" of the majority and thereby has overcome the republican power structure. Looking at the types of 'willing consent' we see the word "interest" is more than a clue for how to organize democratic power.

Anyone hoping to build a democratic power structure must

start by assessing the people's interests. Trust may not work at the beginning because there is not a prior relationship between leader and follower within the context of a democratic organization. Habit will not work because where there has been no democratic organization, there has been no opportunity to develop habits regarding one. The only vehicles for obtaining willing consent at this point are self-interest and common interest. To locate these, you must go door to door and ask people one at a time, face-to-face, about their interests.

There is no technological or marketing substitute for face-to-face contact when you are trying to start a democratically based organization. Willing consent can only be granted via a relationship of one person with another. One or two individuals, canvassing a neighborhood, can build a network of relationships centered around a common project. It is on these relationships that an organization can be built.

To begin, you ask people about their community. What is good about it? What are the bad sides? What would make the community better? How long have they been in it? How did they come to be a part of the community? How long do they plan to remain in it? Do they participate in any of the institutions within the community? Where do they get together with other community folks and what do they do when they are together? What do they think of the services provided in the community (government, business, and non-profit)? What's good? What's bad? What's lacking? Not every person you speak with will be willing to answer all these questions. Some situations will suggest different questions. The point is to engage people in conversations about their community and to listen carefully to what they have to say. From their response you can identify people's self-interests and common interests. Patterns will emerge. The repetition will give you the best hooks upon which to hang an organizational effort. Generally five percent of the households in a crossection of your targeted area will provide a sample of sufficient size to obtain meaningful information.

As you are conversing with people, you also are noting: who

articulates well, who is most observant, who expresses a community spirit, who is the most informative. These are the people to return to when the time comes to begin building the organization.

Contrary to some methodologies of community organizing it is not appropriate to identify the existing community leadership and speak only with them.[26] Such a methodology confines the rest of the people to the role of follower. It thereby minimizes their opportunities for participation and is thus much more republican in nature than democratic. When you are starting a new democratic organization, or the organization is starting a major new campaign, you must begin seeking consents among the masses of the people, not from some pre-defined subset. You must start at the bottom of the power structure to build up a new democratic one. To find potential leaders look for people who's self-image appears to include addressing the issue at hand and who show an inclination to speak with their neighbors.

Having heard from the community's individuals it is also valuable to know where people congregate—churches, schools, parks, bars, clubs, social service or civic organizations. Having identified these locales you should attend each one as a casual participant. Observe what values are expressed, the demographic characteristics of the group, how the event is conducted, who is in charge, who they grant authority to, what is the agenda of the group, how it is financed, etc. You will determine whether there are any institutions which include a majority of the community's residents. If there are any you may want to explore the possibility of collaboration with them after your group has gotten itself established as an effective democratic organization. You will also want to identify the small minority power structures within the community. However, these groups may prove to be an obstruction to the creation of your organization if they compete for the political loyalties of a segment of the community. In both cases, you will learn how the residents act when they function as a group.

Researching documents is a good way to complete an overview of the community. Census data is a good place to start. Newspaper morgues may have valuable information. Are there any books about the community? How much are homes selling for? What is the crime rate? How do the schools compare to those in other communities? The Internet can be helpful here, but it's better to get out into the community and track down the paper because you meet more people and you learn more about how the various institutions work.

With this research completed you'll have a sense of where all the individuals with whom you spoke fit into the community in which they reside. Now it's time to go back and review your interviewing data. There are two key categories of questions to answer:

— what are the concerns people had, how are they distributed across the community, where are they concentrated, which are general, which are local?
— which individuals stood out in the interviews as most likely to volunteer, where do they live, what were their concerns, what community groups do they belong to? Be sure to be wary of those who are active in other organizations that might perceive a new group as competition.

Having answered these questions you want to overlay the answers on top of each other. Where they match is where you'll start to organize.

Who conducts this process of interviewing and research? It could be you and a couple of friends or neighbors. Sometimes it is a hired organizer from an existing organization. If both are available it should be a combination. Follow the steps, listen well, gather support, act as a group and you can get the job done.

If you're beginning from scratch, you'll most likely want to start small. Pick out the most winnable and hottest issues with the best volunteer potential. The issue will be the thing that motivates participation.

Having identified the resources at hand, the next step is to begin the organizing.

THE RITUALS OF DEMOCRACY[27]

INTRODUCTION

". . . the assurance of things hoped for, the conviction of things not seen . . . what is seen is made from things that are not visible." Hebrews 11:1;3

While a bear is hibernating, you'd never know it was there. Once it awakes and reassumes its role, all the other powers in the woods must continually cast a wary eye over their shoulder.

Democratic power, for the most part, lies latent in America's neighborhoods. This lack of use means it is weak and generally ignored. To put democracy to work thus requires "the assurance of things hoped for, the conviction of things not seen". Your vision of a democratically empowered people must remain clear, even though the current reality may consist of isolated and inactive individuals largely unaware of and uninterested in the power they actually possess or the benefits to be derived from exercising it. To give substance to things unseen requires r*itual.*

Ritual is a means of sustaining willing consent. It is similar to habit in that it results from repetition. However, habit is the repetition of a single act by a single person. Ritual requires the repeated participation of a group of individuals in a series of acts and so becomes ceremonial. It gains its significance from the sharing of the repetition. The ritual appeals to the common interest of individuals and creates a bond of trust where one's self-interest is woven together with the community that shares in the ceremony.

There are actions which, when repeated, will lead from individual apathy to active democracy. This chapter lays out those practices, but a leader is necessary to initiate the ritual. That person may well be you, the reader. If sustained, the shared actions can instill a culture of democracy in an otherwise divided and weak populace.

The history of democracy in America is one of highs and lows. At times democracy has been unseen and unheard, while at others it has been a tidal wave mobilizing millions and agitating an entire nation. Throughout time, however, people always have the power. Whether they are awake and using it is another question. If one has confidence and effectively implements the required steps democracy can rule in America.

RITUAL I—IDENTIFYING THE FIRST ISSUES[28]

The community research is completed and it's time to start building the organization. Generally speaking you want to start small and simple.

From hundreds of interviews, you've identified clusters of concerns as well as prospects for participation in the organization. Based on that combination, you know where you are most likely to have success in getting people to agree to come together around a common cause. Now you must find the issues.

An issue (as defined on page 32) is: a tangible and resolvable concern, felt by a majority of the people in a definable population, which they are willing to commit time and energy to resolving.

For example on the 1200 block of Washington Street, you spoke with four people. One of them seemed interested in getting together with her neighbors to clean up the abandoned and burned house three doors from her home. Two of the others also mentioned the house as a concern. There was an additional person on the street behind the house (1200 block of Adams St.) who commented on it during an interview. You also know the local government has a cumbersome, but potentially effective, procedure for addressing this concern.

At this stage you have identified a tangible issue that is resolvable with a reasonable amount of effort on the part of several people working together. However, you've yet to determine whether the concern has the potential to be felt by a majority of the people impacted by it (in this case, those on the block with the building and perhaps those on the block behind it) and whether there is sufficient determination to see it through to the end. In order to answer these questions, you'll need to talk with more people.

Having identified the area of impact, you want to ***knock on the doors*** in the area, and continue doing so until you've spoken with someone in a ***majority of the households***. These conversations will repeat the pattern of the initial interviews, except that, if they don't bring it up first, you will ask specifically about the burned house. Their initiative is a measure of their concern. You want to know how many residents are concerned about this issue, what information they may have, and how much they want to do something about it. If these additional interviews indicate the issue is felt by a majority and a sufficient number of them are willing to commit time and energy to resolve the concern, you're ready to organize.

PROLOGUE TO A CASE STUDY[29]

It was a cold and windy night on the southwest side of Chicago. The once abandoned bungalow had been reoccupied by the son of the owner. The owner had fled to the suburbs to avoid the influx of black residents that was heading his way. There had been trouble ever since the son had moved in. Large drunken parties involving boys attracted by the presence of numerous girls from the Catholic High School several blocks down. It appeared there was some gang affiliation. A car had been set fire in the alley behind the garage. There had been some gunshots fired into the house from the street. This night, however, was going to take the cake.

Several dozen youths showed up for a Friday night party. As the night wore on and the folks got drunker they also got louder. It was hard for the neighbors to get to sleep that night. Some time in the early morning hours the Valdez family on the south side of the bungalow finally drifted off. But they were awoken by smoke and light. Looking out their bedroom window they saw fire flashing out the back attic of the party house, the flames were lapping at their own home. A quick call to 911 got the fire doused and protected their own home from significant damage. No one was injured. The party house sat burned, vacant, and open for days.

RITUAL II—COLLECTING THE FIRST CONSENTS

From all your interviews, you want to identify the people who are most likely to extend themselves for the issue. These folks are the ones who will have a self-interest in the matter (perhaps they live next to the house, or maybe they have children they are afraid will play in the house and get hurt) and an understanding of how their concern also affects the other people in the area (see 'Types of Willing Consent' in Chapter 4). Pick the one who is most likely to consent to work on the issue and go ask them to do something tangible to address it.

What do you ask them to do? The thing that is most necessary to get the ball rolling—in this case, host a meeting in their house or yard. Hosting a meeting means two things: providing a place and inviting participants.

Don't ask them to do all the work. Offer to help put together a flyer and to run the meeting. You might even go with them as they ***ring the doorbells, deliver the flyer to every household on the block, and ask their neighbors to come for the meeting.*** The flyer, in addition to stating the date, time and location, should state the purpose of the meeting: to begin an organization on the block and discuss the burned house.

The flyer should be distributed in the evening or on the weekend (whenever people are most likely to be home) five or so days before the meeting: soon enough so that people won't forget, yet long enough so they can make plans to attend. The ***doors should all be knocked on again two or three hours before the meeting***—to remind people and to catch those who weren't at home the first time around.

CASE STUDY

Christina was home just starting to get ready for a night shift on her job as a nurse when the doorbell rang. It was some guy with longish hair and a beard wanting to ask questions about the neighborhood. She was a little annoyed at the odd interruption and told him she had no time to talk, but she did have one thing to get off her chest—that damn house across the street. It was a lucky thing no one was hurt, but at the rate things were going that was just a matter of time. And that S.O.B. O'Malley who ran to the suburbs cause one 'colored' family moved into the house across the vacant lot from his didn't give a damn about anybody any more. He wouldn't return phone calls and his burned house was just sitting there waiting to cause more trouble.

The organizer knocked on ten more doors after talking with Christina and only three of them had anybody home and answering. Still, he knew he'd be back because two of those three were ticked about the burned house as well. Funny thing was, he hadn't even noticed it when he first came on the block. After pondering matters for a couple of days he decided Christina was the most likely candidate to get something started so he went back to visit her about an hour later than he was there the first time. She wasn't home. Two days later he went by again and caught her heading out the door. Still angry about the house she told him to come back the next day about an hour and a half earlier. When he returned he asked her to host a meeting and pass out flyers. She was hesitant, but said she'd ask her husband.

She told the organizer to come back in a couple of days. He did. She said no, her husband didn't like the idea, but she thought the family renting the top floor of the two flat across the street two doors down from the burned house might host the meeting. If they agreed, she said she would help by passing out the flyers.

So the organizer went across the street and spoke to the wife in the two-flat. Her two kids were jumping up and down singing "La Bamba" which they'd learned from their new friends at school. The wife said they were new to the neighborhood, but had met Christina and thought it was terrible what had happened at that house. She said a meeting was a great idea, but she'd have to ask her husband. Could he come back in a couple of days. Yes, he said and left feeling optimistic but a little disconcerted by the stack of bigoted Nazi literature he'd spied by the wall in the hall next to the bathroom he'd asked to use.[30] Two days later he was back and the wife said yes to the meeting and a date was set.

RITUAL III—ASSEMBLING THE CONSENTS: THE FIRST MEETING

The first meeting will likely be a small gathering. The rituals you undertake will be focused on facilitating a sense of community, building an action-oriented organization, and establishing a pattern of outreach and inclusion—flowing from one stage to the next like a lake swell moving toward shore.

Start by having a host do what a host does: welcome everyone as they arrive and offer a place to sit. Refreshments are a nice touch but generally not essential (this may vary depending on local custom). They'll know it's not a party because the host will also hand out agendas as people enter. Once everyone has gathered the host should ***ask each individual,*** starting with herself, ***to say a bit about who they are and their relation to the block*** ("my name is Andrea Kopytko, I live in the two-flat at 1221 with my husband and kids; we've lived here for six years"). The host should then introduce you as the person who will be conducting the meeting that evening.

The meeting's ***agenda*** should be printed[31] . It should include a *Welcome* (which the host has completed) and an *Introduction* to the purpose of the meeting ('we're here tonight to meet some of our neighbors we might not have known, to create a block organization so that we can get things done for our block, and to talk specifically about the burned house"). The *Principles* by which the organization is proposed to function should also be enunciated:

— we will be 'majority-based' meaning that we will not take on a project until we've checked with our neighbors to make sure a majority of them are in agreement and have given some formal sign of their support.

— we will be 'independent' meaning we will speak and act for ourselves in any contact with people or groups outside the block and we won't align ourselves with any partisan political organizations.[32]

The *Structure* of the local organization should be determined. Simplicity is best for this size and stage of organization. There should be a 'phone tree' listing all those people who have agreed to participate and a handful of agreed-upon 'representatives' who will function as the informal 'go to' people when something needs to be brought before the organization.[33]

With the groundwork laid, it's time to move on to the concerns that drive the organization, in this case the burned house, and set *ActionPriorities.* A good place to start is by discussing what people know and feel. From there, the group should talk about whether they want to try to do something about it and, if so, what that should be. The resolution of that topic could be held for the next meeting or, if people feel sufficiently confident that they are on the right track, they could ***formalize a proposal to be taken to the block*** as a whole. If it is the latter, a motion should be made and voted on and provision made for implementing the decision. In the days following the meeting:

- — someone will need to draft the written form in which the proposal will be taken to the rest of the neighbors.
- — the draft should be reviewed and approved by the representatives to make certain it is consistent with the vote of the meeting.
- — volunteers will need to ***take it to the neighbors at their homes, explain it, and ask them to sign their approval.*** Before adjourning, plans for the *Next Meeting* should be made: date set, location determined, co-chairs from the group selected, volunteers assigned to distribute the invitations by knocking on the doors. That meeting becomes the deadline for completing the signature selection (unless circumstances dictate a quicker turnaround time). The second meeting also sets the plans for implementing the proposal. If the situation is urgent the second meeting might become the point at which the implementation begins, so plan accordingly.

In between the meetings, several things are critical if the organization is to develop on a truly democratic path. First, the volunteers going door-to-door must not just collect signatures, they need to explain the proposal so the people know what they are agreeing to when they sign. It is important to gather signatures from, at a minimum, a majority of the households in the target area—the more the better. The majority support must be genuine.

Second, the person who laid the initial groundwork for the meeting must speak with those who participated to say thank you, gauge their reactions, and offer any interpretation and explanation that is needed.

Third, provision must be made for checking back with the volunteers to make sure the work is getting done and to address any questions or difficulties that arise.

Fourth, a ***pre-meeting*** needs to be set with the person who laid the groundwork and the two co-chairs for the next meeting so they can assess how matters are progressing, prepare the agenda, allocate and define roles, and anticipate and prepare for any difficulties.

CASE STUDY

As the organizer left the first meeting he knew he was onto a good one here. Christina had done a great job passing out the flyers, talking with nearly all the households on the block. The hosts (the Bardis family) had even provided coffee and Lithuanian pastries. Everyone signed up for the phone tree and Christina and Mrs. Vazques were going to take a letter door-to-door inviting Mr. O'Malley to another meeting at the Bardis' house.

These folks were so anxious to get that building cleaned up they wanted to skip the usual second meeting. Co-chairs were selected who, oddly enough, were Charleen (the college age daughter of the new black family on the block) and Peter Bardis (the Nazi whose bigoted literature was not stacked against the wall near the bathroom for the meeting, having been left at doors all across the neighborhood the day before). An older Lithuanian couple, who'd lived on the block since the homes first went up just after World War II, was going to pass out the flyers for the next meeting.

RITUAL IV—THE PRE-MEETING

The pre-meeting to the second meeting is essential. It is at this point that the process of developing new and indigenous democratic leadership begins.

The pre-meeting is the 'dress rehearsal' for the meeting itself. If you want a successful meeting, the spokespeople must be well prepared—"winging it" is an invitation to mistakes. The preliminary results of the signature collection should be reviewed and a proposal for action developed to be submitted to the meeting. It is best to bring an actual proposal so there is something concrete to which people can react. An open-ended, spur-of-the-moment discussion would likely result in a poorly conceived plan. The various elements of the meeting should be divided by agreement among the two co-chairs.

Having two co-chairs is important, whenever possible, for three reasons:

— they can support each other during the meeting
— if one is unexpectedly unable to show up (remember, these folks are volunteers) there is someone ready to step in
— it enables more than one person to have the experience of conducting a meeting, therefore increasing the potential spokesperson resources.

RITUAL V—DELIVERING THE CONSENTS: MEETING WITH THE 'TARGET'

Having assembled the consents of a majority of the households, it is time to ***approach those with the means to resolve the issue.*** In the current example of a vacant and fire-damaged house the "target" is likely to be a government agency. A designated spokesperson and a delegation, composed of as many residents who can possibly attend (striving for maximum possible participation is nearly always the best policy), should go to the agency and deliver the signatures with a cover letter explaining exactly what is being requested. Since democracy is people power it is important that the action request be made in person whenever possible.

It is often suggested that the first request should be addressed to the elected representative. While not crippling this is a mistake nonetheless. If the people are to be truly sovereign, then they need to address their request to the person who actually must do the work to fulfill it—intermediaries only serve to dilute the authority of the People. Elected officials are public servants. Their appropriate role is to support the demonstrated opinion of the majority. The proper contact to the elected official would be a copy of the request and a statement that, should a problem arise with the agency, the people will contact the elected official to enlist his/her support in obtaining the proper response. The initiative should always lie with the people.

If there is an established government procedure for addressing the concern, then making the request (inspect the building, cite appropriate violations, initiate enforcement procedures) *and* obtaining a timeline for its fulfillment is sufficient. A designated representative should contact the responsible agency official when the deadline has arrived to determine the status of the anticipated action. If the agency fails to carry out the requested action then a meeting should be sought. It must be clear that ***failure to respond is not an acceptable occurrence. Repeated failure should be met with appropriate tactics of persuasion, protest, or coercion*** (the determination of which is beyond the scope of this case study). The people are sovereign. Having faith in that concept and acting accordingly will eventually assure success.

If there is no established procedure, then an invitation to a meeting should be the initial action. The purpose of the meeting is to explain the issue and obtain an agreement regarding a process to address the concern.

Whether there is an established procedure or not, the block should follow a few clear steps in order to effectively engage the agency:

— have a designated spokesperson
— have the group gather together before entering the agency office to a) review the purpose of the action; b) ensure that no additional issues, which have not been through the process of gathering majority consent, are brought up; c) obtain agreement that anyone speaking other than the spokesperson will speak only in support of the agreed upon position; any disagreements will be discussed afterward, not in front of the agency

— enter as a group, speak as a group, leave as a group (the strength is in the group; splitting the group in any way reduces the effectiveness of the action)
— debrief immediately afterwards.

If the group is going to the agency to initiate an established procedure steps two and four can be conducted outside of the agency office. If the agency is coming to the meeting, the agency should be invited to come a half hour after the meeting actually begins (there should be provision for a waiting area if they arrive early) and should be asked to leave before the meeting concludes.

CASE STUDY

Everything was set. Charlene and Peter had met together in Peter's house with the organizer for the pre-meeting. It had gone well, they agreed upon their roles, and they seemed determined. The Lithuanian couple hadn't done quite as well getting the flyers out as Christina had, but she had taken the initiative to call everyone on the phone tree the night before to remind them. Twenty people were in the flat, Charlene and Peter had briefed everyone on the plan for the meeting and O'Malley was to arrive (the letter having been sent return receipt requested and Christina having actually confirmed O'Malley's attendance on the phone) in five minutes.

A half hour later O'Malley wasn't there. Christina went to call. The old Lithuanian couple left in disgust. The Bardis kids had begun singing "La Bamba". Christina returned and said O'Malley's younger daughter had told her he'd gone to visit his sister in the next suburb over. The neighbors were angry and self-incriminating—"we're wasting our time thinking we can get him to do anything about this". The inwardly downcast organizer suggested that they compose a note expressing their frustration and drive to O'Malley's new house and deliver it. The thirty minute drive each way was not an inducement. Charlene was trying to get people to compose the letter. Two or three folks were listening.

The others were grousing. Then Ms. Vasquez said, "I'd sure like to give him all that burned wood from his house lying in my yard." "Great idea!" exclaimed the organizer. "We could dump it in his yard and tape the note to it." This made a lot of folks uncomfortable, but the idea helped the residents regain focus and a debate issued. Peter took a vote—10 to 8, let's do it. Charlene finished the letter. Six people left. The rest signed the letter while Christina went to get her van. The organizer suggested they make copies and distribute them to O'Malley's neighbors.[34] The group agreed. Peter offered the use of his xerox machine to make the copies. Ms. Vasquez went to get the burned wood. Everybody and everything was loaded up into the van and headed to Palos.

In the van on the way folks were chuckling about how Peter and Charlene would make quite an impression on the O'Malley family. After all, he'd moved all the way to Palos without even selling his house in order to get away from Charlene and her mom. When they pulled up in front of the nice new split level home on the Palos cul-de-sac it was raining. They dumped the burned wood on the muddy parkway and went to ring the doorbell. Low and behold O'Malley himself answered the door. Peter said hello and Charlene said they had a letter. Everyone stepped onto the nice white shag carpet while Charlene read the letter. O'Malley was beat red with anger. Peter showed him the copies of the letter they were going to go give his neighbors. That really set O'Malley off. Christina suggested that if O'Malley would agree to repair the house and sell it perhaps they wouldn't need to explain to his neighbors why they'd left that pile of burned wood in his front yard. O'Malley, looking straight at Charlene said he'd do it, but they better not ever come bother him in his new home again. The group returned to the van. During the ride home they reviewed the evenings events and made plans for their next steps.

The next day Christina utilized the phone tree so everyone would call the Alderwoman (a decision made despite the organizer's advise to call the agency) to get the building inspected. With a dozen angry phone calls all demanding immediate action,

Ald. Carter responded quickly. The inspectors were out the next day. The next week contractors were out starting work. The organizer, stopping by the Bardis' to see what they thought of the progress, found Charlene babysitting their two kids. Four months later the repaired home was sold to the block's second black family (he was a cop, she was a teacher). There were no more late night parties. The Bardises moved to a Palos apartment when their lease was up.

A RITUAL FOR THE CONSECRATION OF LOCAL DEMOCRACY

The rites of local democracy inculcate and enforce the sovereignty of the people: the people gather together, act together, and are thereby empowered. The ritual steps, when followed, manifest a relationship with a greater reality. Individuals, formerly isolated and weak, find themselves to be part of something larger. Their participation with their neighbors will improve the quality of life for the community as a whole. The sum is greater than its parts.

The steps emphasize communication among the people for the purpose of developing a majority consensus. To work, the steps of the ritual must be repeated for each gathering of the people. With repetition, the ritual will enable the organization to grow in power and gain results.

The People Gathered

- knock on the doors of a majority of the households
- ring the doorbells, deliver the flyer to every household on the block, invite each neighbor to attend
- knock on the doors again two or three hours before the meeting
- ask each individual to say a bit about who they are and their relation to the block

The People Act

- create agenda
- formalize a proposal to be taken to the block
- take it to the neighbors at their homes, explain it, and ask them to sign their approval.
- hold a pre-meeting

The People Empowered

- approach those with the wherewithal to resolve the issue.
- persuade, protest, or coerce to achieve an acceptable response.

Failure to respond by the target of the people's action is not an acceptable response. Repeated failure requires the people to mobilize more power in order to obtain the necessary response.

may have once been strong but now find their leadership core diminished. Blocks just beginning to get organized will have a level of resources and experience to draw upon that the initial blocks did not. As is generally the case, the whole is stronger than the parts and the parts will benefit from the stronger whole.

There are three elements necessary before moving from the collection of distinct block organizations you and your neighbors have established to a community-wide organization:

- — critical mass. The majority principle is a good guide here too. You want an organization on half or more of the blocks in the target area. This will provide the pool of participants from which the larger organization will be built.
- — indigenous leaders. These are the people who have been conducting the block meetings and speaking with their neighbors door-to-door (don't assume the same people will always be fulfilling both roles).
- — one or more neighborhood issues.

When you have the first two elements in hand it's time to identify the third. The rituals are very similar to those involved in starting the block meeting, except more people are involved.

RITUAL VI FINDING THE COMMON CONCERN AMONG THE BLOCK ORGANIZATIONS

There are many ways in which you can find the common concern among several blocks. The choice depends on the circumstances. There are occasions when a neighborhood wide concern is so prevalent it cries out to become an issue (see page 32 for a definition of issue). In this case you can simply call a meeting to begin developing the concern into an issue. Under different circumstances you may identify a common concern simply because it has become an issue or been suggested as one at a large number of block meetings. Perhaps there is an event that is new and requires quick action. In such a circumstance you can test whether it has issue potential by applying the door-to-door process outlined for single block (see pages 50-51) to a crossection sampling the community. Sometimes it's not at all clear what common concern might lead to a unifying issue. This is the hardest case so we will begin with it.

Rather than going door-to-door to identify the issue go block-to-block. The block leaders should first get together to agree to implement a process for consulting each block organization. The process should be simple so that it can be repeated similarly on each block. Akin to a focus group, it would contain the following steps:

— call a meeting on each block (the block meeting rituals should be repeated)

— include in the agenda an explanation from the leader that the leaders of various blocks have decided to consult each block organization regarding concerns that impact the whole community.

— ask those present at each meeting three questions: "What is the one thing that you most want to change in our neighborhood? What is the one thing that you most want to see protected? What is the one thing the neighborhood doesn't have that you think it most needs?"

— ask the questions one at a time. Each person will write down his own answer. The leader will then ask each person to state her own answer. All the answers will be written down on a common sheet. The group will then discuss the answers and vote on the one best answer for the whole group. This process ensures that each individual, no matter how quiet by nature, has a voice. It also ensures that the individuals decide as a group.

— repeat the process for each question. At the end, the block has a single answer for each of the three questions.

CASE STUDY

The organizer was beginning to recognize the symptoms of burnout in himself as he prepared to bring the results of the focus groups to the block clubs' first joint planning meeting. The focus groups had seemed endless. The same questions over and over again. The same answers to the same questions: these jerks painting graffiti on the side of our homes need to be sent away; parents need to take responsibility for their gangbanging kids; they're shooting at each other on the next block over; we've called the cops but the punks are still here. The frustration and sense of powerlessness was palpable in all the meetings. Would anyone come to the next night's post-focus group planning meeting? Would all these seemingly demoralized block clubs really be able to form something bigger and successfully challenge the criminal forces threatening their community safety? It didn't seem so. Clearly the issue would have to be the gangs. How could they define it and what was the solution? It was time to start thinking vacation—four day weekend, yes.

Then the phone rang.

It was Rita Svenson from the 5200 Troy block club. There were ambulances and cops all over the parking lot at Rico's Tacos behind her house. The place had become a hangout for the Kings. This had great implications as Rico's was in the territory claimed by the Ambrose. The last few weeks had brought lots of flashed gang signs, a few fights, and rumors of attempted drive-bys. Rita had even had one of the fights enter her home as several foulmouthed Kings had chased a lone Ambrose through her back door and out the front. For the organizer, who'd been halfway out the office and on the way home, it was a fast drive to Rico's.

The whole place was sealed off with bright yellow crime scene plastic strips. There were cops and a crowd. The ambulance was gone. He didn't recognize any of the cops, but there were a few familiar faces in the crowd. Rosario was there from over on Albany. She was usually good at getting the facts right so he walked towards where she was standing staring across the yellow strips. As he approached he was pulled up short by the site of the remnants of a huge puddle of blood ten feet on the other side of plastic over near the alley. He knew it was bad. He knew he wouldn't be taking any vacation. He knew, if he did his job, people would be at tommorow's meeting.

There were tears in Rosario's eyes. From her he learned that Jimmy O'Conner, a fifteen year old who had been rumored to be a King wannabe, had gone over to challenge a car full of Ambrose driving slowly through the alley, a gun had come out the backseat window and it was the blood from Jimmy's head all over the asphalt. He had lived at the other end of the block from Rosario. Would she be at the meeting tomorrow night? Yes. Would she call her block club phone tree to tell them what had happened and remind them about the meeting? She'd already done that before the shooting. Yes, but it's different now. We've got to stop this. Will you call again? Yes.

The organizer looked around. Jorge Quintanilla, who'd hosted the new block club meeting over on Whipple, was talking with someone near the cop car. He went over to talk with him. There was anger and despondency written all over Jorge's face. This was what Sally had predicted would happen at the focus group meeting. Had he made his reminder calls to his phone tree? No. Would he go home and do it. He was too sick to his stomach. It was time to consider moving. Jorge, people are dying, we need to act. Make your calls. Jorge said he'd think about it and turned towards home.

After speaking with a few other people he knew, the organizer left the scene. It was nine at night, but he went ringing doorbells. Every block representative who would answer the door was given the news and the request to call their phone tree. The gangbangers had been the chief topic at nearly all of the focus groups. He heard the same complaints about do-nothing cops, bought-off alderman, and lazy residents but there was a change in his people's eyes as he mentioned the blood in the parking lot. It looked like some unmade phone calls were going to be made.

His last stop was Bill Evertowski. Bill was the guy who had

reluctantly agreed to chair the next night's meeting. He'd just met with him that afternoon to plan out the agenda. Bill had lived in the neighborhood nearly all his life. He was disgusted with the changes that had come in recent years and blamed it largely on the influx of Mexicans. Still, he had a knack for leading small groups and he tended to rise above his own shortcomings on those occasions. There were hints in some stories that Bill might have done some minor gangbanging himself while growing up in Back-of-the-Yards—perhaps he was so angry about what he was seeing because he knew from whence he spoke. Bill was asleep, but his middle aged son who was still living at home agreed to wake his dad up.

Bill was angry at being awoken. "This had better be damn good or you ain't ever seeing me at one of your meetings again," he shouted as he sat on the couch. It wasn't good, but it was important. They had a couple of beers and talked about the neighborhood and the meeting. They scrapped the agenda—the plan to carefully review the focus group results and to suggest a petition drive that was to demonstrate majority support for an anti-gang initiative by the cops. Events had provided "focus" for the focus group results. They would propose a march and silent vigil at Rico's Tacos. They would strive to show majority support with bodies instead of signatures. They would pull people together, march to the site of the murder (and the King's hangout), and show the gangbangers that the community would not be intimidated. Bill was pissed.

Without dinner but with three beers in him the organizer was a little buzzed as he drove home after midnight. Still he knew it was a damn good thing they'd done all those focus groups. He had eighty people who had spoken with each other about the gangs, he had a dozen who had shown some tentative leadership attributes, and he had a phone network that could quickly spread the word. He didn't sleep well that night, but he was in to work early the next morning.

RITUAL VII—CONNECTING THE BLOCKS

The group of block leaders will gather together to count the votes of the blocks and discuss the results. They will select the concern on which to focus. The decision should be based on the breadth and depth of the expressed concerns. A meeting will be called to discuss the concern selected. All the participants in the block organizations will be invited to attend. The group of people will develop a report (which may take more than one meeting and some outside research to complete) containing two items:

— a clear, concise, and brief (a few sentences) statement of the concern and its importance to the neighborhood
— a proposal for how to address it.

With the report in hand the group of block leaders will call a community meeting. All residents of the target area will be invited to attend. Repetition is the key to an effective community invitation. At a minimum, flyers should be delivered to all the doors, and all those who have participated in the block organizations should receive a reminder phone call. The more additional ways the invitation can be delivered, the more likely it is people will know about the meeting and consider attending.

The group will present its report to the community meeting. After a discussion, a vote on the proposal, including any amendments, will be taken. If approved, volunteers will be sought to take the statement, in the form of a petition, letter, or ballot, door-to-door where it can be explained and people can sign it. The goal will be to collect enough signatures to represent a majority of the households in the community. Once that goal is attained, it is time to take the proposal to the target—whomever has the wherewithal to address it.

CASE STUDY

It was a planning meeting like no other. Thirty people were present.

They were angry at the gangbangers, angry at the cops, and angry at themselves. Bill had a hard time containing the discussion.

The proposal for the march met with approval although some were afraid to so directly challenge the Kings turf as they feared retaliatory bullets. The date was set the next week—almost everyone agreed to pass out flyers; a delegation would obtain the alderman's presence for the march; Bill would ask Father Mike to join in the march; another delegation would ask the police district commander. The march would start at the church and head down Kedzie to Rico's, pause for a prayer and a speech, and return to the church.

Jorge, however, was not satisfied. He was insistent that a march, good as it might be, was just a one time deal. He wanted more. Gangbanging went on every week he said. Did people really believe a march and a prayer would stop that? He was right, everybody knew it, but it was nine o'clock, people were tired, the spirit of determination was deflating. The organizer was feeling desperate.

Bill saved the day. He told the group how, as a kid, he and his friends used to fight with the Irish a few blocks over. After one particularly bloody fight involving baseball bats and switchblades the Holy Name Society from his parents Parish went door-to-door talking with all the parents. It put a big damper on the fights, and it led to Bill dropping out of the gang. Bill suggested trying the petition drive that he and the organizer had decided to scrap the night before.

Rosario complained that a march and petition drive was just too much work. The organizer, however, was prepared for that reaction. He suggested that the group ask Father Mike, in his prayer at Rico's, to pray for the neighbors to go out and speak with their neighbors about the violence and for the police to work to stop the gangbanging. Bill, in his speech, would then propose a petition drive calling on the police to make graffiti, loitering, and other symptoms of gang activity their top enforcement priority in order to avoid a repeat of the escalation of little incidents that led to the murder. A voice vote would be taken and a group from the planning committee would fan out among the crowd with forms and pencils so as to recruit an additional set of volunteers to conduct the petition drive.

It was agreed, and the residents were excited. A followup meeting was set for the next month when plans would be made to deliver the petitions.

RITUAL VIII—OPEN "COMMITTEE" MEETINGS

As the issue develops, there will be a need for ongoing discussions and decisions about the actions necessary to obtain victory. Decisions should be made in open 'committee' meetings where all those who have been part of the previous discussions or expressed interest via informal conversations with leaders or staff are invited (if you're not inviting many more than actually attend, you're not inviting enough people). The agendas for these meetings will be determined by discussions among the leaders (those who have led meetings and spoken with their neighbors) on the 'committee'. It will be essential to make a provision for periodic communication to the entire community regarding the status of the issue. Opportunities to facilitate community participation should be seized—phone blitzes on a recalcitrant target, group actions at a target's office, community meetings held at critical junctures such as when a 'target' is invited to address the topic, issues placed on the ballot as referenda, etc..

CASE STUDY

The march had been a stunning success. Two hundred people had gathered in the Parish Hall (the location selected so that it would be possible to get everyone's name, address, and phone by funneling the entire group by a table in front of a single door as the entered). After Rosario had called the group together and given instructions on how the march would proceed they had headed into the dusk with Bill, Rosario, and Jorge leading the way along with Father Mike and the alderman. The only no-show was the police commander though he did insure that patrols cars preceded and followed the crowd as they walked slowly down the street to Rico's Tacos. When Bill proposed the petition drive it was met with a resounding cry of support and enough people volunteered to cover nearly 90% of the blocks in the neighborhood. While some gang members had been seen observing the march from a distance and flashing signs the immediate impact was to clear out Rico's Tacos for several weeks and quiet the random fights and gunshots that had begun to plague the community.

After the march, preparations were made to prepare for the first "Stop the Gangs Committee" meeting—letters had been sent out and nearly 1,000 petitions had been collected from the fifty blocks and the public and parish schools. The Commander had reluctantly agreed to a meeting in his office the following week. At the pre-meeting (prior to the Committee meeting) the organizer suggested to Bill, Jorge, and Rosario that the organization design a survey whereby the block clubs and other residents who had come forward since the shooting would identify gang hot spots. The Commander would be asked to commit to making those areas his top priority and to providing court data regarding any arrests that were made. A court watch program would be initiated so that residents could attend and insure adequate prosecution. The leadership trio agreed to make the proposal at the meeting.

As the Committee meeting got underway forty people were present. Bill outlined the plan agreed to in the pre-meeting. "That no good Commander ain't gonna agree to this," was the first comment that came from the crowd. "He didn't even come to the march and he's never agreed to give us arrest records before." True enough. The organizer should have anticipated this reaction, but he hadn't.

"What do you suggest we do if he says no?" Bill asked.

"Ain't nothing you can do," was the response. "He's the Commander and we can't give him orders."

"How about another march only this time to the police station," said Jorge. "If the cops are gonna let the gangbangers off they're as much a problem as the lousy hoods."

"No one's going to march on the cops. We'd all get busted. What, do you think they'll let us block their door with a bunch of signs saying they're no good like the gangs? Never happen," said John from 5900 Spaulding.

"Yeah, Father Mike'd never be up for this one," said a lady from the back the organizer couldn't identify.

"We gotta do something if he stiffs us," said Bill looking straight at the organizer. "Help us out."

"How about a community prayer service in the police station parking lot," he said. "We'd pray for peace and a new spirit of cooperation from the police. Extend our hand, offer them our support."

Without any better alternative, yet knowing there needed to be a fall back plan, the Committee voted to accept the proposal. Everyone figured they'd better make sure they did a good job of getting the Commander to agree to the demands cause if he didn't their position would not be a strong one.

Spokespeople were chosen. Special roles for people who had particularly grievous gang crimes happen on their blocks were assigned. Representatives from the few blocks that had already assembled specific data were selected. Volunteers who had collected the petitions to be delivered to the Commander would testify to their readiness to distribute and collect the surveys. All would speak so that the Commander would be forced to realize the problem was severe and an effective solution was before him. An organizational infrastructure sufficient to enforce community accountability would be made obvious by the testimony of the volunteers.

It was a hard package to resist. After the Commander's initial doubts were rebuffed by Jorge, who was the chief spokesperson, he agreed.

Once again volunteers spread across the community distributing information and collecting survey input. The majority was mobilized. The officials were responding. The gang activity ultimately dispersed to the surrounding communities.

* * *

Since ritual is important to the long term success of building the community identity that sustains a democratic organization, it is important to note the ritual forms for assembling consents as they are conducted at this stage of organizational development:

— leaders consider plans for expansion and solicit input from general participants (focus groups)
— a plan developed by leaders to address issues raised by participants is submitted for discussion and vote at a community meeting (in this case the march)
— the plan as approved is taken door-to-door (petitions)
— the structure of open committee meetings is established to provide for ongoing work on the issue.

At every stage, plans developed by a small group of residents are brought to increasingly larger groups of residents for discussion and approval until a broad cross-section of the entire community has been involved and its consent obtained.

This same process of building a larger neighborhood organization from smaller block organizations can be repeated so that the neighborhood organizations are combined to form a neighborhood federation. At each stage, the power of the residents is increased by the larger number of consents they are able to gather and the greater material resources they are able to assemble to further their efforts. The time it takes to create such an organization will allow for numerous repetitions of the rituals of democracy. The organization and its democratic mode of functioning will have become integral to the community. With continued success it will be a form of democratic government paralleling the republican one.

To attain such a level of success and complexity your organization will need a number of experienced leaders and staff. It is therefore important to pause and consider the qualities of leadership and staff that will be necessary.

RELUCTANT LEADERS

"The Lord said . . ."you shall bring my people Israel out of Egypt." "But who am I", Moses said, "that I should . . . bring the Israelites out of Egypt? . . . I have never been a man of ready speech, never in my life."

—Exodus 4:10-11

"You know that in the world the recognized rulers lord it over their subjects . . . That is not the way with you; among you, whoever wants to be great must be your servant . . ."

—Mark 10:42-43

"Where every man is a . . . participator in the government of affairs, not merely at an election one day in the year, but every day . . . he will let the heart be torn out of his body sooner than his power be wrested from him by a Caesar or a Bonaparte."[35]

—Thomas Jefferson, letter to Joseph Cabell, February 2, 1816

To succeed any ritual needs someone to lead the participants through its steps. Those people are your leaders. A good democratic leader will, initially, be reluctant. Having grown into the role she will see herself as a servant to her community. Once fully mature she will know that the most central virtue is not winning the issue but assuming and exercising liberty and defending it from the Bonapartes of the world.

Like Moses most leaders are at first uncertain of their abilities, averse to the impending responsibility, or doubtful of the likelihood that people will grant them the authority of a leader. Each of these concerns are precisely the attributes that need to be developed in order to exercise effective leadership. An individual must be aware of what he lacks in order to gain the knowledge necessary to grow and be effective. Through experience a new leader will gain the confidence to assume responsibility and by ably assuming responsibility she will earn the people's grant of authority.

Individual choice is not the primary element of becoming a leader.

Charisma is not the first prerequisite. The cult of personality is not effective. Lone rangers need not apply.

Leaders are called to the role by grants of authority from their fellows and chosen by the ordinary circumstances of day-to-day living. If they appear larger than life it is because the whole is greater than its parts and they are a symbol of the whole. To be great, one must serve. Leadership is a partnership with other leaders and a service to those who are led.

If you are to build a democratic organization you must either identify potential leaders and guide them as they grow into the role, become a leader yourself, or both.

How do you find the leaders on which to build an organization? Trial and error. Once you've identified the jobs that need to be done you begin to ask individuals to do them. The leaders will eventually emerge from among those who actually do the work. Leaders are generally those who do the most and do it the best. It is in the action that they learn and develop.

The best ones will grow into it and make it their own.

Who makes a good leader? Someone who understands she is part of a larger whole. Someone who is humble enough to know her shortcomings yet confident enough to challenge her teacher.

Ideal community leaders will have five qualities: they must be a member of the community the organization is seeking to represent, they must be able and willing to work, they must be able and willing to engage their fellows (at the door, during meetings), they must approach the task as a form of service to their community, and they must get a sense of personal satisfaction from the overall effort.

The flipside of this list constitutes the qualities to avoid: loyalty to community democracy is compromised by competing loyalties, people who talk a good line but don't show up for practice, people who won't both listen to and take a stance among their fellows, people acting primarily from egotistical or selfish motivations, and people who don't care about addressing community issues with their fellows.

Leaders are not pure. They will not perfectly match all the five criteria (or perfectly avoid the five negative criteria). To become the best, leaders must strive:

— to learn and think critically; accept constructive criticism and be willing to take risks. They must work via action and reflection; action, reflection.
— to be ready to be out front and willing to hold up the rear.
— to be able to share, to step aside (temporarily and, eventually, permanently) and make room for others to grow.

Just as leaders must learn and grow, they must also be concerned with the growth and maturing of the organization, not just with winning issues. Therefore they need to:

— provide opportunities for others to become leaders
— pass on their knowledge to others
— recruit volunteers
— work as partners with, and evaluators of, any staff
— help raise money.

Ultimately leaders are defined by three things:

— the authority their fellows grant them as key figures in a democratic organization (not by the number of people they can bring to a meeting)

— their willingness to make a long term commitment of their time and talent to the organization.

— their readiness to make room for others so that the authority of leadership remains dispersed among the people.

People who lead in this fashion stand squarely within the Republican tradition which was the ideological soil of the nation's founding. It's a tradition that speaks of honor more than rights.

Honor is an old concept, worthy of reflection. It connotes a sense of duty, implies a readiness to work, assumes your self-worth is somewhat determined by your worth to others, and proclaims a willingness to risk for the sake of principle. It is no accident that the "Medal of Honor" is generally given to those who risk their lives for the sake of their fellows.

Jefferson often spoke of the "natural aristocracy"—those who would rise to the top from amidst the day-to-day functioning of society. Like Jefferson, who wrote the Declaration while preoccupied with the home he'd had to leave, these are reluctant leaders—servants of the people. Individuals who place the common good above personal profit and who, in the long run, are surprised to find they are better off for it.

HONORABLE CITIZENS: THE PREREQUISITE FOR DEMOCRACY

"Honor—esteem, respect, reverence; personal integrity maintained without legal or other obligation." [36]

Jefferson's claim that a person who is a regular participator in public affairs would rather have his heart torn out than lose the authority he is accustomed to exercising is an inspiring statement. It also illustrates the dilemma faced by 21st Century patriots.

The corollary to Jefferson's maxim might be: those unaccustomed to regular participation in public affairs will not recognize the power they have and will slip complacently into a benevolent tyranny masked by a democratic facade.

Examples of this corollary abound in Chicago where there is no longer any organized partisan alternative within the local 'republic,' and the Democratic party organization has access to taxpayer resources to reward its 'volunteer' canvassers (precinct captains) with jobs and its donors with contracts. In addition, citizens or citizen organizations, having no comparatively viable organized political alternative, partisan or otherwise, must depend on the munificence of the local boss of the Democratic party who is in turn dependent upon the Mayor, for access to public resources. Such an extreme concentration of control in a few hands means local activists will rarely disagree with city officials for fear of jeopardizing whatever access they still possess. "Political activism" and cozying-up to the alderman become one and the same thing. When such a subservient attitude becomes the political norm, cooption rules. Chicago is a one-party state masquerading as a republic.

If you look across the country you will find many other local communities dominated by one party or the other. As the saying goes, "Don't make no waves; don't back no losers." Somehow it's just not as inspiring as "where every man is a participator in the government of affairs, not merely at an election one day in the year, but every day."

Compounding this lack of access to political authority is the pernicious loss of democratic aspirations among the citizenry. The reduction in participation is exhaustively documented in Robert Putnam's "Bowling Alone" (see 'Afterward'). The trend is unmistakable. People are consenting to allow others to make decisions impacting their collective life. Where this view dominates in local communities, special elites will consolidate their power and gain the greatest portion of the benefits of the commonwealth. As the practice spreads across the nation the framework for political decision making increasingly shuts out the people—elections are decided not by counting the votes, but by judicial fiat; international trade agreements grant cliques of corporate and bureaucratic interests the ability to overrule decisions made by duly elected representatives. The democratic soul of the American erodes within this stifling framework.

To counter the dilemma posed by complacent and docile residents 21st Century patriots will need to cultivate honorable citizens.

Honorable citizens are those who will invest themselves and do so consistently. If democracy is about power exercised by people, then there is no democracy if the people are not active.

An honorable citizen votes, reads the newspaper, grants

authority to a civic organization, donates money, participates in some form of organized activity that provides a tangible community benefit, expects government and corporate entities to be accountable to her community, and protests when they are not.

An honorable citizen is a participant. There is no democracy without active participation. If government is ignoring the people, there can be only one reason—the people are ignoring the government.

Our elected elite will obey the people only when the people provide instructions. Do we really expect our politicians to have a pollster call us on the phone while we're watching "Baywatch" or the "West Wing", and then do what we say they should? If we always vote for whoever the precinct captain recommends will the politicians ever have to worry about losing an election? If all we do is vote every four years, do we expect the elected elite to provide anything more than lip service during the other three? What if we don't even vote?

As a citizen, to what authority are you consenting to obey?

An honorable citizen holds the democratic process in high esteem and fulfills his patriotic duty to participate. Because democracy is won in the mundane details of volunteer work squeezed into an already hectic life, those of us who are involved must get those who aren't to rejoin.

There are things your organization can do to encourage participation.

The **first** thing is to **ask** citizens to participate. When you ask you must provide some information. Education is critical. What do you want him to do? Why should he do it? You will also need to ask in a variety of ways. This is true for two reasons. One is that different people respond to different things. The other is that repetition is critical if your suggestion is to be understood and validated.

You will ask a lot of people. If you want fifty there, you'd better ask at least five hundred.

Asking numbers is also important for more than just turnout. When you're asking you're also educating. Each contact is about gaining consent, a request for authority. That person may never come to one of your meetings. But when a volunteer knocks on their door to ask for a signature they'll be more likely to get it; when your issue is on the ballot you'll be more likely to get the vote; when the topic comes up over the fence or in line getting groceries, you may gain support—a grant of authority. The little places are important too. If a hundred people show up for your meeting and your issue is a topic of conversation in the community then the nominal authorities know they must pay attention, they must respond.

After asking, you must **involve**. People must be given something to do. They must feel a sense of belonging. Democracy is not something you can do alone. There are innumerable little tasks involved in the practice of democracy: attendance is the most basic, but anything that people can do together which furthers your cause is fine. However, you don't want to stop there. If people are going to exercise power they must be involved in making decisions. There must be ways for them to do so.

If you want to build majorities you cannot wait for the people to come to you, thus the need for door-to-door conversation and mechanisms of decision making for the masses.

Surveys are a good tool. "What should we do with that vacant lot? Here's five options we've heard discussed. Rank them." Petitions are time tested. "Our survey told us people wanted a library. Here's why. We want to tell the City this should be a budget priority. If you agree, sign here." Notice you're not just getting a signature, you're also educating and listening. A petition is a tangible demonstration of dialog and consent. Just as a politician's petition to get on the ballot is an essential part of the electoral process, a community's petition represents a critical piece of democratic decision making.

Referenda carry the authority of a vote "Shall the City build a library". Obviously binding is better than advisory, but use what you've got available. Any actual vote requires a campaign, which means you'll be out engaging the populace and involving them in the decision.

You must also have those who do attend anything help make decisions. Your volunteers need to grow to become mature practitioners of democracy. Participants, some of them anyway, must become leaders.

Watch for those with a particular interest or who prove to be reliable volunteers. Invite them to planning discussions or committee meetings. Solicit their ideas. Ask them to speak at public events or in meetings with outside parties. Each act of participation verifies the organization you are trying to build. *Share the authority to implement the decisions made by the majority.*

Third, you must **affirm** people when they participate. Like involvement this must be done broadly among the masses and particularly with individuals. Getting articles in the local newspaper is an excellent way of recognizing what your organization has accomplished. It makes people feel important. Your own newsletter should celebrate your accomplishments and highlite especially significant individual contributions. Parties, festivals, and banquets are great places to award both individual contributions, celebrate collective accomplishments, and affirm dedication.

Individuals need to be recognized as well. Simple thank yous are important. A phone call with a word of appreciation and a brief comment on the significance, however small, of the task done will reap future benefits. A handwritten note or small gift are also good forms of recognition.

Affirmation is the means by which you remind people that what they do is important. It's sharing and bonding—two things essential for any kind of collective endeavor.

This task of finding and mobilizing honorable citizens is made all the more difficult by the general lack of established local democratic organizations. Without any frame of reference it is often difficult to understand even the concept of a majority-based citizen initiative much less put it into practice. Assuming the initial effort is successful, there will be the challenge of institutionalizing the process. Repeated experience and the establishment of democratic rituals will be critical. People will need to decide to move beyond the issue that first engaged them and to move beyond their own block or small aggregation of blocks on which they began.

Taking these critical early steps can be greatly aided by the presence of a professional organizer, trained in the practice of majority-based organizing. In the end, however, it all comes back to the decisions individuals make about whether or not to become involved. All the tools for facilitating democracy can be in place, but if people don't step forward the elite will rule.

When people expect their local government will respect their sovereignty, when opinions are expressed in an organized fashion, and when people react when government fails, that will be the day the government will begin to obey. Whenever the majority of citizens act consistently in such a manner the government will almost inevitably obey.

Democracy is not about freedom. Freedom is a by-product of democracy. It is what happens after all the hard work. Freedom is like money—if you want it, earn it. Democracy lives only when citizens honor it with their participation.

PROFESSIONAL ORGANIZERS

The work of building a local democratic organization is work that can be done by volunteers alone. You can start with your own determination, a partner or two, and the resources available in your community. However, if you are going to build beyond a few blocks and if you want your organization to be around for many years, you will need to have staff. You'll have bookkeeping and clerical work to get done, but most importantly you'll need a good organizer. There are four reasons why.

First, the entities which your organization is confronting have full time staff, more than you'll ever be able to have. All government offices are run by folks who do their work full time. Most elected officials have people paid to assist them. Certainly corporations, businesses, and most non-profit agencies have paid staff. If your organization hopes to remain effective and maintain its independence in the rough and tumble of political competition, it will need full time staff to support it's volunteer leadership.

Second, when you build a house you hire a contractor. When you build a citizens' organization you hire an organizer. There are skills and talents that can be developed by doing full time professional work. If you want to have an effective organization you will want to have the resource of professional organizing available.

Also, as is exhaustively documented by Robert Putnam in "Bowling Alone,"[37] fewer and fewer Americans are participating in civic activity. With less experience comes less knowledge. You'll need staff to help your citizen volunteers develop the skills of democracy.

Finally, one of the factors affecting the drop in participation documented by Putnam is a reduction in time available for volunteering. Longer commutes and double-income families mean less time for community. While this is not a central factor it is a significant and legitimate one. Staff support can enable your organization to function in a more timely manner.

What does an organizer do? An organizer doesn't do the organization's work; she gets other people to do it.

A good analogy is the college coach. For example, an effective organizer will:

— recruit participants, assesses their skills and appraise their potential in order to put them in the position from which they can make the maximum contribution to the team effort.
— train volunteers to improve their skill level and learn new ones.
— push your volunteers to stretch and grow.
— plan and design strategy and the tactics of implementation.

When it comes time to play the game the organizer stands on the sidelines and the volunteers go out to win or lose.

The key difference between the organizer and a coach is that the organizer must do all these things in partnership with the volunteer leaders. The ultimate authority does not lie with the organizer, but with the participants. An organizer can't order anyone to do anything, but must see that the work gets done nevertheless. An organizer is both a servant and a partner.

An organizer must set aside his own issue priorities and focus on those of the community for which he works. An organizer must be able to provide objective advise regarding issues, strategies, and tactics. Therefore it is important that, whenever possible, the professional organizer not live in the community for which he works. This is what distinguishes them from leaders. Like the organizer the leader is a servant, though one who is passionate about the issue that is driving the community's effort. Where there are no organizers, the leaders must also bear the often conflicting burden of providing objective analysis. Being at once passionate and objective is a prescription for burnout. Organizers thus have a silent but critical role in preserving active participants and thereby enabling them to remain honorable citizens.

An organizer's job is much more difficult than a coach's. Our democracy is more important than a football team. Yet the pay scale isn't in the same league as a coach's. An organizer must be motivated primarily by a belief in people and a commitment to their empowerment. There is just not enough money available to properly fund democratic organizations. Nevertheless your organization should strive to pay a livable wage for the work it receives.

"LAWS OF NATURE AND OF NATURE'S GOD"

"We hold these truths to be self-evident, that all Men are created equal, that they are endowed by their Creator with certain unalienable rights, that among these Rights are Life, Liberty, and the Pursuit of Happiness."

Thomas Jefferson, as is clear from the Declaration's appeal to "the Laws of Nature and of Nature's God", was a student of nature. His claim that human rights were "endowed by [the] Creator" illustrates that liberty was, in his mind, somehow intrinsic to human nature. He went on to claim that the democratic processes emerging in his day were a response, perhaps an outgrowth, of this nature: "to secure these rights, governments are instituted among men, deriving their just powers from the consent of the governed."

The words of the Declaration were representative of a common perspective during the days of the revolution when it was widely felt that " . . . everyone in the community was linked organically to everyone else"[38] and "'the happiness of every individual' depended 'on the happiness of society.'"[39] Viewed politically, this line of thought meant that "the private liberties of individuals depended upon their collective liberty".[40] This revolutionary era perception that democracy was somehow integral to the human condition deserves more credence than it is typically given today.

In modern language, democracy may well be an evolutionary response to the modern human condition—a development of the cooperative instincts that go all the way back to our species' hunter/gather origins.

Human evolution is uniquely complicated because people have freedom, the ability to make conscious choices. In the words of Edward O. Wilson human evolution is a "gene-culture coevolution". He describes culture as "the communal mind" and says "in this respect human beings differ fundamentally from all other animal species."[41] In other words humans, collectively, may decide to differ from their genetic path or may decide to develop their genetic instincts along paths that natural selection, operating as it does with other species, might not have taken. The choice is collective, not individual, and as such the acts that will constitute that choice are inherently political—the gaining, maintaining, and directing of collective consent. The choice for, or against, democracy is a central one for the future of the human race.

Humans are social animals. The functioning of our society is the essence of who and what we are. Like ants and wolves, our society is composed of a complex web of relationships. Without those relationships we would not exist. The deep history of the human animal contains within it a process of communal decision making and action that is intrinsic to the survival of our species.[42] This reality is so basic to our nature that it is likely built into not only our social and psychological makeup, but even our genetic code. We became human as small communities of semi-nomadic hunters and gatherers. Mutual dependence was a reality that was taken for granted. Decisions were made collectively. Our species has evolved, culturally and genetically, within that framework. If it is true that our survival as individuals is dependent on the survival of the group, then our political structures should take that mutual dependence into great account.

Unlike ants and wolves, humans have the ability to decide to alter their patterns of behavior. Each individual has the freedom to decide what she is going to do. This freedom is both a curse and a blessing. It enables humans to act in ways that are inemicable to the equality into which we have been created. Hierarchical power structures in which society's ability to get things done is utilized for the benefit of an elite are a result of this choice. Human freedom also enables individuals to choose to act in accordance with the perception that all people are created equal.

Democratic power structures, in which a people's ability to get things done is utilized for the benefit of the many, are a result of this choice.

The mutual dependence of individuals upon each other is at the core of the democratic concept of how power functions. If we are social animals then we are most likely to get things done by acting together for our mutual benefit. Failure to adequately take such a truth into account would likely result in a peril to the overall health of the human race. If correct one would expect there to be discernible consequences. Although there is little, if any, scientific work directly addressing this topic there is one recent report regarding research done in Chicago which can be considered. It sheds an interesting light if viewed from the angle described above.

The report, "Neighborhoods and Violent Crime: A Multilevel Study of Collective Efficacy" looks directly at how a failure to account for mutual dependence can negatively effect community life. Its definition of collective efficacy, "social cohesion among neighbors combined with their willingness to intervene on behalf of the common good", is similar to the definition of democracy—people governing society directly. Sampson, et. al. go on to say their study focuses on "the effectiveness of informal mechanisms by which residents themselves achieve public order". They conclude "collective efficacy . . . accounted for more than 75% of the variation between neighborhoods in levels of violence".[43]

While far from scientific proof, this suggests that at least one example of illness in our society, violence, can be traced to the lack of power that people have over their day-to-day living. One might reasonably infer that creating a community power structure focused on peoples' natural state of dependence and need for cooperation would contribute to a reduction in neighborhood violence and other problems associated with dysfunctional communities.

If America is to stop the deterioration of its community life it will need to provide a means for its people to directly address the violence, selfishness, isolation, and factionalism that pervades our contemporary society. This is something that can only be accomplished as a group and is therefore preeminently, though not exclusively, a political question. The answer lies in the creation and utilization of democratic institutions of parallel government.

AFTERWARD

Academia has discovered the decline, and the need for regeneration, of civic participation among Americans. It's reality is being documented and it's causes explored. This trend is well illustrated by Robert Putnam's study, "Bowling Alone." His key finding that, " . . . more than a third of America's civic infrastructure simply evaporated between the mid-1970's and the mid-1990's",[44] is supported by impressive documentation and confirmed by the day-to-day experience of community activists across the country. His book does an excellent job of illuminating the outlines of our national malaise.

Putnam cites several causes for this decline. He attributes 10% of it to "special pressures on two career families", another 10% to suburban sprawl and commuting, 25% is attributed to television, and the remainder he allocates to "generational change—the slow, steady, and ineluctable replacement of the long civic generation by their less involved children and grandchildren . . ."[45] This last one begs the question as much as it answers it.

Putnam's explanations of the decline generally focus on things that have happened to us, as though the decision's of many not to participate in civic life were little influenced by rational choice. There is another explanation. Perhaps people have chosen not to participate in civic life mainly because it wasn't working.

The nation's political structures, rather than helping to facilitate the influence of the collective voice of the people, have actually served to restrict it. That reality has left the private associations, so touted by de Toqueville, virtually impotent. Many Americans have simply gotten tired of beating their heads against the proverbial brick wall. The country doesn't need more of the same old forms of civic engagement. It needs new methods and organizational forms faithful to America's rich democratic past yet adapted to overcome the contemporary power elites.

Putnam argues the "long civic generation" was greatly influenced by the national unity instilled in Americans during World War II.[46] The generation that has quit participating, however, got it's start being sent to fight a war many thought was wrong. The civic structures to which the previous generation had been so committed now seemed as likely to be enemies as allies. "Four Dead in Ohio"[47], was a generational anthem regarding everyday students shot dead by people wearing the same uniforms the previous generation had worn to defend freedom. The protests were not heeded. The war continued to drag on even as a majority came to oppose it. The children of the rich and the powerful often did not have to serve, much less fight and die. Those who did fight were not honored. Told they were fighting communism they found themselves propping up a corrupt puppet regime with little popular support. When they returned, their sacrifices for freedom went ignored. And then came Watergate—the President flagrantly breaking the law for personal political gain.

Suddenly government's failure to solve community problems while local political insiders kept raking in the juicy contracts, not to mention the outright graft, was no longer an unfortunate exception to the rule, it was part of the larger pattern of political life. The cynics, it appeared, were right. Volunteering for the common good was a fool's game. "They" don't listen to the People, but only to the well-healed and well-connected. It isn't a matter of a loss of trust by millions in their civic institutions, it's the fact that those institutions are too often unworthy of our trust.

Putnam offers a number of solutions to the decline of social capital which begin with the phrase "Let us find ways".[48] While not bad ideas, they are feel good solutions which presume that generally good people once alerted to the problem of declining participation will wake up and start correcting the problem. What Putnam, along with most Americans, doesn't see is that the decline of civic participation is a question of power. We've lost because others have won. We've quit playing because it isn't clear how we can win.

Distant elites and their bureaucratic minions have taken over the decision making authority in our nation. We are left standing alone and powerless, fleeing from our problems via ever lengthening commutes to a comfortable sofa where we can sit on our butts and watch TV. The American revolution has been bought, consumed, and left like a crumpled can lying by the side of the highway. The people have become the minions. America is developing a slave mentality.

It doesn't have to be this way. People will participate when they see that their participation might get something done. We need an understanding of how we can regain power over our community lives. We need to rekindle faith in the American creed of the sovereignty of the people. We need to tap the repressed anger of years of shame and frustration borne of political failure and impotence. We need to get off our butts, stand together, build organization, learn how to take control, and then do it—it's the American way.

—Clayton Daughenbaugh, Berwyn, IL, USA 2001

APPENDIX ONE

THE SAVE OUR CITY COALITION PRINCIPLES AND PHILOSOPY OF LOCAL DEMOCRATIC ORGANIZING

1. A local democratic organization at all times seeks to represent, act on behalf, and attain the support of the majority of residents of the community it serves.
2. It strives to be inclusive of the entire community (and not just select segments such as church members or ethnic groups).
3. The purpose of a community organization is to empower the people of a community with the "know-how" and political capability to manage, control, and take responsibility for their present and future.
4. Information must be provided through a variety of channels to all community residents to insure that consensus is achieved, independence maintained, and representation real.
5. It builds upon and strengthens those attributes, values, and hopes that make the people of a specific community "unique".
6. Organizational issue positions are established by mechanisms which can demostrate the support of a majority of local residents (such as petitions, surveys, and ballots)

and must be seen as part of a whole process of organization-building, not as ends in themselves.

7. Leaders are committed to and appreciate the necessity of involving and instilling confidence in local residents to participate in the affairs of the organization. As spokespeople, they represent the majority view of their community. With other leaders, they work in a spirit of cooperation and reach decisions collectively.
8. Boards of Directors have a fiduciary responsibility for the organizational infrastructure (money, staff, office) and a judicial responsibility to insure organizational compliance with democratic principles.
9. Staff respect the communities they work for, provide, the technical skills for organization-building, and are an essential resource for all the people of the communities they serve.
10. Coalitions are formed with equals in size, philosophy, and objectives.
11. Funding strives to achieve local self-sufficiency.
12. Leadership and staff must view each other as partners with different roles but similar goals of service on behalf of their communities.

The goal is to establish independent democratic organizations of neighborhood governance that will become institutions paralleling the other private and public organizaitons and institutions within the community.

Independent meaning:

— not allied with individual political candidates or electoral organizations
— issue agenda set by the citizens not by any other organizational or financial relationships
— able to raise sufficient funds by its own efforts to insure organizational survival without any outside funding

Democratic meaning:

— core decisions regarding issue priorities will be made by the people themselves and will not be delegated to representatives via elections or to paid staff
— the sole source of issues will be the concerns expressed by community residents
— the organizations will strive to demonstrate majority support among those voting age residents residing within the area impacted by the issue ('strive' because few votes' really involve the majority of those eligible and most organizations don't build in a maximum effort to seek majority support as these will).

Neighborhood meaning:

— the organizations will be geographically based and layered with block clubs combining into neighborhood organizations combining into a community federation combining into an inter-community or regional coalition. Theoretically these layers could continue to the state or national level. In any case, to be effective, there must be a corresponding organizational and programmatic structure at each layer that functions within the framework of the model.
— membership will be determined in a fashion similar to citizenship in a country, you need only be a voting age resident of the community to have a right to participate in the 'legislative' processes of the organization.

Governance meaning:

— there will be an established "legislative process" whereby the people can set priority issues for their community and, via sub-entities such as open committees, provide for ongoing issue campaigns designed to win issues. This process will include arenas of public discussion such as community meetings and mechanisms for community ballots such as petitions, surveys, or advisory referenda.

— there will be an executive and judicial function fulfilled by a Board of Directors that shall provide oversite to insure the organization is in compliance with the 'Model' and with relevant laws and regulations and to rpovide oversite of the organization's personnel, financial, and physical resources.
— there will be communication networks to provide for community education and input
— there will be training for volunteer participants provided by professional community organizers

Parallel meaning:

— most private entities are composed only of segments of the community and most governmental entities are either bureaucratic or representative and are therefore not democratic
— organizations functioning in accord with the model will likely be the only truly democratic entitites in the community
— the means of holding other entities accountable to the community.

A community organization is more democratic as it directly involves a larger number of people (ideally a majority) in a level of decision making regarding their community and it enables citizens who have previously held little or no community authority to become leaders in their community.

APPENDIX TWO

VOLUNTEER LEADERSHIP

WHAT IS A LEADER?

— an individual who promotes and participates in the right of the majority to set policy priorities for his/her community
— an individual who sees his/herself as a member, representative, and servant of the community and a partner with other leaders and staff within the organization
— an individual who guide's, and/or sets an example for, the implementation of the organization's planned activities

HOW DO INDIVIDUALS BECOME LEADERS

— by fulfilling opportunities, given to them by the organization, to carry out roles involving leadership
— by participating in reciprocal relationships with other leaders in which they offer each other praise and constructive criticism
— by receiving and implementing training and guidance from professional organizers

WHAT ARE EXAMPLES OF TYPICAL ROLES PLAYED BY LEADERS?

— run meetings, speak with the media, meet with outside "officials", lead actions, coordinate volunteers, encourage participants, educate and solicit support from individual members of the community (often done at the doorstep), conduct fundraisers, etc.

APPENDIX THREE

STRUCTURE AND DYNAMICS OF A COMMUNITY ORGANIZATION

PRINCIPLES

— represents a majority perspective of constituents
— invites everyone to participate
— maintains political independence (i.e. does not align itself with any partisan political organizations)
— seeks accountability to the community from government, business, etc.

STRUCTURE

"Executive"

BOARD OF DIRECTORS

— sees that principles are applied in all aspects of the organization
— coordinates the acquisition and maintenance of resources (staff, office, and money) necessary to run the organization
— maintains proper legal standing of organization
— speaks for organization in absence of Committee

leadership or when enforcing the application of organizational principles

STAFF

— prepares and advises for all aspects of organizational activity

"Legislative"

COMMUNITY MEETINGS

— authorize organization positions on community-wide issues
— initiate demonstration of majority support (petition drives, etc.)

ISSUE COMMITTEES

— coordinate organizational activities addressing community wide concerns; meetings are open

BLOCK WATCHES

— coordinate above activities on specific block(s)

ROLES

LEADERSHIP: run meetings, handle media, meet with 'outside' rep's., lead actions, coordinate volunteers, encourage participants, conduct fundraisers, etc.

VOLUNTEERS: collect signatures, distribute literature, assemble mailings, make reminder calls, attend meetings, assist fundraisers, etc.

STAFF: prepare, support, and give guidance to leaders and Directors; recruit, prepare, and coordinate volunteers; run office

OPERATIONAL INFRASTRUCTURE (ideal)

BOARD

1, or more, representative from each Committee
1 representative from each Sector (may double as Committee rep.)
1 representative from each participating institution (if any)

COMMITTEES

2-5 leaders
15-30 volunteers
up to date list: new people added regularly; non-attendees weeded out annually

BLOCKS or SECTORS

2-4 leaders
6-20 volunteers
1-2 meeting places
"phone tree"—regularly updated

INFORMATION DISTRIBUTION & SIGNATURE COLLECTION NETWORK

Flyers & Letters: generally focused on a single issue or event; often distributed to targeted areas or constituencies
Newsletters & Newspapers: generally cover multiple issues and events; distributed across entire community — both types announce, inform, & persuade to take specific action(s) (ex. attendance, phone call)
Distribution: every block (3 times a year)
Collection: 3/4's of blocks (twice a year)
1 mailing to entire neighborhood each year
distribution & collection at each church & school several times a year

STAFF

consultant, organizer(s): provide technical skills and serve as resource

PREPARATION FOR ORGANIZATIONAL ACTIVITIES

COMMUNITY MEETINGS

— planning meeting 3-4 weeks prior (sets agenda, begins to line-up leaders and volunteers, plans turnout)
— turnout
-bulk mailing (200, or more, pieces) 2 weeks prior
-door-to-door flyering (done 3-4 times a year) begins 6 days prior
-flyers distributed at churches and schools 2-6 days prior
-reminder phone calls 2-3 days prior
-announcements at other groups' meetings 1 month, or less, prior
—briefing
-of leaders 2-5 days prior
-of volunteers 1-5 days prior

COMMITTEE MEETINGS

— consult leaders on agenda and letter 10-14 days prior
— turnout
-1st class mailing (less than 200) 7 days prior
-reminder calls 2-3 days prior
— brief leaders 2-3 days prior

BLOCK or SECTOR MEETINGS

— consult leaders on agenda (if not determined at a previous meeting) and flyer 10-14 days prior
— brief leaders 2-5 days prior
— turnout
  -1st class mailing 7 days prior
  -door-to-door flyer distribution 3-6 days prior
  -reminder phone calls 2-3 days prior

ROLES FOR A COMMUNITY MEETING

— Chair: instructs crowd, introduces speakers, moderates discussion, and takes votes in accordance with the agenda
— Speakers: address assigned topic
— Floor Team: supports agenda, chair, and speakers from crowd
— Ushers: welcome and direct crowd, control disruptions, inform Chair and Speakers of the arrival of Guests, collect and distribute information as needed, set up & take down
— Sign-In: get name, address, & phone of those in attendance

AFTER THE MEETING

— de-brief with leaders and staff: what did we do right? what did we do wrong? what did we get? what did we lose?
— thank you's to all volunteers
— call a sampling of attendees, particularly those who showed potential to become volunteers: thank them and ask their opinion
— inform the community (here's what we wanted, here's what we got, here's what it means) via flyers, letters, newsletters, and newspaper articles

GETTING, AND KEEPING, INDIVIDUALS INVOLVED

The Three Part Cycle

— ask, inform, motivate *in person and in writing*
— involve: give them something to do that they can do and can grow from
— thank / update: in person (thanks for whatever they did and tell them it was important; if someone you really wanted there, or is normally there, wasn't; they need to be updated)
— repeat cycle cointinuously

Keep Good Lists

— who has participated (name, address, phone, email)
— what activity they participated in (attendance, flyering, phone calls, mailings)
— what issue has been the focus of their participation.

APPENDIX FOUR

DEVELOPING A STRATEGIC PLAN FOR WINNING AN ISSUE

— what is the issue and how do you know it is one? (an issue is a winnable and tangible concern, felt by a majority of the people, of whom sufficient numbers are willing to see it through to the end, which the effort to address will serve to build democratic organization within the community)
— how will you personalize the issue? (a helpful exercise here is to compose a simple story about the issue's significance in the life of individuals and/or the community)
— how will you demonstrate that the issue has the majority support of the community?
— who are your initial spokespeople?
— who is the target? (who can 'deliver' what you need in order to win the issue)
— who is the opposition? (maybe, maybe not, the same as the 'target')
— how will you inform & involve the community during the campaign?
— what strengths and weaknesses does the opposition bring to the issue; how will you take advantage of the weaknesses and counter the strengths?
— what strengths and weaknesses does the organization bring

to the issue; how will you utilize the strengths and correct, or compensate for, the weaknesses?

— what tactics will you employ to get the 'target' to do what you want?

— how will the issue help develop the organization? (new leaders, new participants, new money)

— do you have the money to pay for the planned activities; if not, can you get it; if so, how?

— develop a six month workplan (what specific actions will you take when)

APPENDIX FIVE

AN ORGANIZER'S JOB

(the items listed under each category are examples, they are not meant to be exhaustive)

Listening:

what are each person's concerns for the community?
where does each person fit into the community?
how does each person view other individuals in the community?
what groups of people does each person identify with in the community and what is their opinion of them?
how does each person view authorities and institutions in the community?
how does each person view their community's relationship with surrounding communities?
who articulates concerns and opinions in a way that represents their neighbors?

Observing:

where do people come together and what role does that play in their lives?
what activities do most people carry on as individuals and where?

what things tend to confirm or contradict the cumulative opinions learned from listening?
what institutions impact, for good or ill, the concerns and values of residents?
what institutions/organizations, if any, in the community involve a majority of residents?
what are the housing patterns in the community and how do institutional forces effect them?
who do people look to as informed about conditions and concerns on their block, in the institutions and groups to which they belong, and in their community?
who does volunteer work?

Building Relationships: Trust and Accountability

do what you say you will do when you say you will do it
provide accurate and sufficient information
ask and prepare individuals for specific tasks and duties
followup to address any difficulties and to identify opportunities for growth
balance requests for participation with respect for other time commitments
use name only with permission
keep informed
seek feedback
ask for opinion and information

Preparing:

clearly explain the role and task requested
practice with the volunteer where necessary
provide advise and information necessary for completion of role and task
allow enough time for information to be "internalized"

Teaching Key Democratic Principles:

all power and authority emanates from 'the people'
political power is the result of individuals acting as a united and disciplined group

Agitating:

remind people of:
- what they have at stake
- what they can accomplish through collective action
- the consequences of inaction

affirm inclinations to action and solidarity

Articulating:

identify common concerns and give them, orally and in writing, expression in a clear, dignified, and (where necessary) forceful manner that people will recognize and/or adopt as their own

APPENDIX SIX

AMENDING DEMOCRACY INTO THE CONSTITUTION

Section 1: Every ten years each state shall establish Township boundaries so that no Township has more than 12,000 voting age citizens and no less than 10,000 and shall provide funding for the functioning of the Townships. The boundaries shall be as contiguous as possible conforming to natural geographic features.

Section 2: Each state shall establish rules of order for its Township assemblies or delegate rule making authority to its Townships.

Section 3: Each Township shall call meetings open to all registered voters at least three times a year to discuss the public business and shall every other year elect a chair, vice-chair, treasurer, and secretary who may serve no more than five consecutive terms. These officers shall not be affiliated with any partisan political organization seeking to elect representatives to any legistlative or executive body in the federal, state, or local government. All registered voters shall have a right to vote when present.

Section 4: Each Township shall have the right to place up to three resolutions on the ballot at the time of each congressional election whereby the people may vote to advise their elected representatives on the public's business.

Section 5: If a majority of Townships in a state or municipality vote to place a resolution on the state-wide ballot at the time of any congressional election, that resolution shall be placed on the ballot and, if a majority of those voting cast ballots in its favor it shall become law, subject to constitutional authority.

Section 6: The Townships, via the statewide resolution process, may place federal constitutional amendments on the ballot. If two-thirds of the states approve such an amendment in balloting spread over not more than five consecutive congressional elections, the amendment shall become part of the Constitution.

APPENDIX SEVEN

EXCERPTS FROM THOMAS JEFFERSON'S LETTERS DESCRIBING THE 'WARD-REPUBLIC'

. . . the term republic means a government by its citizens in mass, acting directly and personally, according to rules established by the majority; and that every other government is more or less republican, in proportion as it has in its composition more or less of this ingredient of the direct action of the citizens. Such a government is evidently restrained to very narrow limits of space and population. I doubt if it would be practicable beyond the extent of a New England township. The first shade from this pure element, which, like that of pure vital air, cannot sustain life of itself, would be where the powers of the government, being divided, should be exercised each by representatives chosen either for the occasion, or for such short terms as should render secure the duty of expressing the will of their constituents. This I should consider as the nearest approach to a pure republic, which is practicable on a large scale of country or population. And we have examples of it in some of our State constitutions, which if not poisoned by priest-craft, would prove its excellence over all mixtures with other elements; and, with only equal doses of poison, would still be the best. Other shades of republicanism may be found in other forms of government, where the executive, judiciary and legislative functions, and the different branches of the latter, are chosen by the people more or less directly, for longer terms of years, or for life, or made hereditary, or where there are mixtures of authorities, some dependent on, and others independent of the people. The further the departure from direct and constant control by the citizens, the less has the government of the ingredient of republicanism.

If, then, the control of the people over the organs of their government be the measure of its republicanism, and I confess I know no other measure, it must be agreed that our governments have much less of republicanism than ought to have been expected; in other words, that the people have less regular control over their agents, than their rights and their interests require. And this I ascribe to a submission of true principle to European authorities, to speculators on government, whose fears of the people have been inspired by the populace of their own great cities, and were unjustly entertained against the independent, the happy, and therefore orderly citizens of the United States. Much I apprehend that the golden moment is past for reforming these heresies. The functionaries of public power rarely strengthen in their dispositions to abridge it, and an unorganized call for timely amendment is not likely to prevail against an organized opposition to it.

On this view of the import of the term *republic* we may say with truth and meaning, that governments are more or less republican, as they have more or less of the element of popular election and control in their composition; and believing, as I do, that the mass of citizens is the safest depository of their own rights and especially, that the evils flowing from the duperies of the people, are less injurious than those from the egoism of their agents, I am a friend to that composition of government which has in it the most of this ingredient.

—to John Taylor, May 28, 1816

. . . . No, my friend, the way to have good and safe government, is not to trust it all to one, but to divide it among the many, distributing to every one exactly the functions he is competent to. Let the national government be entrusted with the defense of the nation, and its foreign and federal relations; the State governments with the civil rights, laws, police, and administration of what concerns the State generally, the counties with the local concerns of the counties, and each ward direct the interests within itself. It is by dividing and subdividing these republics from the great national one down through all its subordinations, until it ends in the administration of every man's farm by himself; by placing under every one what his own eye may superintend, that all will be done for the best. What has destroyed liberty and the rights of man in every government which has ever existed under the sun? The generalizing and concentrating of all cares and powers into one body, no matter whether of the autocrats of Russia or France, or of the aristocrats of a Venetian senate. And I do believe that if the Almighty has not decreed that man shall never be free, (and it is a blasphemy to believe it,) that the secret will be found to be in the making himself the depository of the powers respecting himself, so far as he is competent to them, and delegating only what is beyond his competence by a synthetical process, to higher and higher orders of functionaries, so as to trust fewer powers in proportion as the trustees become more and more oligarchical. The elementary republics of the wards, the county republics, the State republics, and the republic of the Union, would form a gradation of authorities, standing each on the basis of law, holding every one its delegated share of powers, and constituting truly a system of fundamental balances and checks for the government. Where every man is a sharer in the direction of his ward-republic, or of some of the higher ones, and feels that he is a participator in the government of affairs, not merely at an election one day in the year, but every day; when there shall not be a man in the State who will not be a member of some one of its councils, great or small, he will let the heart be torn out of his body sooner than his power be wrested from him by a Caeser or a Bonaparte. How powerfully did we feel the energy of this organization in the case of embargo? I felt the foundations of the government shaken under my feet by the New England townships. There was not an individual in the States whose body was not thrown with all its momentum into action; and although the whole of the other States were known to be in favor of the measure, yet the organization of this little selfish minority enabled it to overrule the Union. What would the unwieldy counties of the Middle, the South, and the West do? Call a county meeting, and the drunken loungers at and about the court-houses would have collected, the distances being too great for the good people, and the industrious generally to attend. The character of those who really met would have been the measure of the weight they have had in the scale of public opinion. As Cato, then, concluded every speech with the words "Carthago delenda est," so do I every opinion, with the injunction, "divide the counties into wards." Begin them only for a single purpose; they will soon show for what others they are the best instruments.

—to Joseph Cabell, February 2, 1816

. . . let us provide in our Constitution for its revision at stated periods . . . that a solemn opportunity of doing this every nineteen or twenty years, should be provided by the Constitution; so that it may be handed on, with periodic repairs, from generation to generation, to the end of time, if anything human can so long endure. This corporeal globe, and everything upon it, belong to its present corporeal inhabitants, during their generation. They alone have a right to direct what is the concern of themselves alone, and to declare the law of that directions; and this declaration can only be made by their majority. That majority, then, has a right to depute representatives to a convention, and to make the Constitution what they think will be the best for themselves. But how to collect their voice? This is the real difficulty. Here, then, would be one of the advantages of the ward divisions I have proposed. The mayor of every ward, on a question like the present, would call his ward together, take the simple yea or nay of its members, convey these to the county court, who would hand on those of all its wards to the proper general authority; and the voice of the whole people would be thus fairly, fully, and peaceably expressed, discussed, and decided by the common reason of the society. If this avenue be shut to the call of sufferance, it will make itself heard through that of force, and we shall go on, as other nations are doing, in the endless circle of oppression, rebellion, reformation; and oppression, rebellion, reformation, again; and so on forever.

—to Samuel Kercheval, July 12, 1816

BIBLIOGRAPHY

Alinsky, Saul, *Reveille for Radicals*, New York: Vintage Books, 1969.

Goodwyn, Lawrence, *Democratic Promise: The Populist Moment in America*, New York: Oxford University Press, 1976.

Kazin, Michael, *The Populist Persuasion*, New York: Basic Books, 1995.

Matthews, Richard, *The Radical Politics of Thomas Jefferson*, Lawrence: University Press of Kansas, 1986.

Putnam, Robert, *Bowling Alone: The Collapse and Revival of American Community*, New York: Simon & Schuster, 2000.

Rustin, Bayard, *Strategies for Freedom*, New York: Columbia University Press, 1976.

Sharp, Gene, *The Politics of Non-Violent Action: Part One—Power and Struggle, Part Two—The Methods of Non-Violent Action*, Boston: Porter Sargent, 1973.

Slayton, Robert, *Back of the Yards Council: The Making of a Local Democracy*, Chicago: University of Chicago Press, 1986.

Tocqueville, Alexis de, *Democracy in America*, trans. George Lawrence, ed. J.P. Mayer, New York: HarperPerennial, 1988.

Wilson, Edward O., *Consilience: The Unity of Knowledge*, New York: Alfred A. Knopf, 1998.

Wood, Gordan, *The Creation of the American Republic: 1776-1787*, Chapel Hill: University of North Carolina Press, 1998.

ENDNOTES

1 Guillermo O'Donnell, "Horizontal Accountability in New Democracies," *Journal of Democracy,* July 1998.

2 Gordan Wood, *The Creation of the American Republic,* (Chapel Hill: University of North Carolina Press, 1998) p.476.

3 Adrienne Koch and William Peden, eds. *The Life and Selected Writings of Thomas Jefferson* (New York: Random House, 1993), 612. Letter to John Taylor, May 28, 1816.

4 Ibid, p. 613.

5 Koch, 604. Letter to Joseph Cabell, February 2, 1816

6 Richard Matthews, *The Radical Politics of Thomas Jefferson* (Lawrence, KS: University Press of Kansas, 1986).

7 Robert J. Sampson, Stephen W. Raudenbush, Felton Earls "Neighborhoods and Violent Crime: A Multilevel Study of Collective Efficacy" *Science,* August 15, 1997.

8 C. Kim Cummings, "Regenerating Social Capital in Urban Neighborhoods"*Journal of Applied Sociology,* 2000 (vol. 17, #1).

9 Wood, p. 516.

10 Lawrence Goodwyn, *Democratic Promise: The Populist Moment in America* (New York: Oxford University Press, 1976) p. 33. This book is the source of all the cited information regarding the populists.

11 Gene Sharp, *The Politics of Non-Violent Action: Part Two—The Methods of Non-Violent Action* (Boston: PorterSargent, 1973) pp. 424-5.

12 Severyn Bruyn on the back cover of Sharp's *The Politics of Non-Violent Action: Part Two,* "he examines the American

Revolution . . . and claims . . . that the violence . . . was not necessary". While Sharp does not directly make this claim the essence of the argument can be found on pages 337-8; 424-5 of Sharp's book.

13 Michael Kazin, *The Populist Persuasion* (New York: Basic Books, 1995) p. 137.

14 Bayard Rustin, *Strategies for Freedom* (New York: Columbia University Press, 1976) pp. 12 - 14.

15 Robert Slayton, *Back of the Yards Council: The Making of a Local Democracy* (Chicago: University of Chicago Press, 1986) pp. 207 - 210.

16 Alexis de Tocqueville, *Democracy In America*, trans. George Lawrence, ed. J.P. Mayer(1969; New York; HarperPerennial, 1988), p. 190.

17 from the masthead of Sierra magazine

18 Madison, in Federalist X, offered a carefully reasoned argument for a republic over a democracy: "The friend of popular governments never finds himself so much alarmed . . . as when he contemplates their propensity to this dangerous vice (the violence of faction). By faction, I understand a number of citizens . . . united and actuated by a common . . . interest, adversed to the rights of other citizens . . . When a majority is included in a faction, the form of popular government . . . enables it to sacrifice to its ruling passion . . . the rights of other citizens . . . [A] pure democracy, by which I mean a society consisting of a small number of citizens, who assemble and administer the government in person, can admit no cure for the mischiefs of faction . . . A republic, by which I mean a government in which the scheme of representation takes place . . . promises the cure for which we are seeking . . . [T]he great points of difference between a democracy and a republic are: first, the delegation of the government . . . to a small number of citizens elected by the rest; secondly, the greater number of citizens, and greater sphere of country, over which the latter may be extended . . . and it is this circumstance principally which renders factious combinations less to be dreaded . . . Extend the sphere, and you take in a greater variety of parties and interests; you make

it less probable that a majority of the whole will have a common motive to invade the rights of other citizens . . . "

19 Contrast Madison's view of how to protect the rights of the people with that expressed by Jefferson in his May 18, 1816 letter to John Taylor (Koch & Peden), " . . . the mass of the citizens is the safest depository of their own rights and especially, that the evils flowing from the duperies of the people, are less injurious than those from the egoism of their agents."

20 A good source of information regarding possible exceptions is the Neighborhood Funders Group and their publication The *Community Organizing Toolbox* (Washington, DC: 2001).

21 A segment of society, perceived to be disadvantage in relation to the larger society, is more likely to be the recipient of those philanthropic grants given to organizing efforts. While such grants are of clear benefit to local communities, these communities, when combined together, do not constitute a majority. The collective impact of this priority within the foundation community serves to reinforce the split between the lower and middle classes. This perpetuation of the division of the people into minority factions is anti-democratic. As Saul Alinsky argued in "Rules for Radicals" (p. 184) "[the middle-class] is where the power is. When more than three-fourths of our people . . . are middle class, it is obvious that their action or inaction will determine the direction of change." To exclude these people from grants for organizing is to condemn the people to a perpetually marginal political status.

22 Saul Alinsky, *Reveille for Radicals* (New York: Vintage Books, 1969) p. 86.

23 The current model of Industrial Areas Foundation (the IAF is the non-profit founded by Saul Alinsky) has accentuated the trend towards republican structures with its great concentration on "congregation-based" organizing. If pursued to its logical conclusion this method will transform the IAF into a special interest group for churches.

24 Samuel Chase quoted in Gordan Wood, p.371.

25 Gene Sharp, *The Politics of Nonviolent Action: Part One - Power and Struggle* (Boston: Porter Sargent, 1973) p. 26. Sharp's book

contains an excellent explication of the general role of consent in power politics which has influenced this chapter.

26 Saul Alinsky says in *Reveille for Radicals* (New York: Vintage Books, 1969, pp. 64 & 65), "The only way you can reach people is through their own representatives or their own leaders. You talk to people through their leaders . . . "

27 Credit for the concept of applying ritual to the practice of grassroots democracy goes to Mike Smith, Director Emeritus of the Institute for Community Empowerment. The description here is my own.

28 the key elements of each ritual are in bold

29 A composite of several true stories. Since they are from the author's experience they are written from the perspective of a paid community organizer. This is not meant to imply that the initial steps of building a democratic organization can be done only with the help of an organizer. When an organizer is present s/he should generally encourage the people themselves to carry out the actual steps of the ritual. See the 'Professional Organizers' chapter for a description of the role.

30 An organizer, in working to unite a community around common concerns, must respect the right of individuals in that community to hold their own opinions, no matter how distasteful the organizer may find them. In this case, as often occurs, the resident grew beyond his prejudice as a result of sharing a common activity focused on a common concern—a vivid example of the power of democratic action to change the lives of the individuals who engage in it.

31 WELCOME AND INTRODUCTION
PRINCIPLES OF ORGANIZATION: majority-based; independent
STRUCTURE OF BLOCK CLUB: phone tree; 'representatives'
ACTION PRIORITIES: discussion; vote
IMPLEMENTATION: draft proposal to take to block; volunteers to knock on doors
NEXT MEETING: when, where, co-chairs, flyerers
ADJOURN

32 A democratic organization should not align itself with a republican one because their fundamental objectives, like oil and water, don't mix. A republican organization is focused on getting power from

people and granting it to particular individuals. A democratic organization is focused on retaining power among the people. With such an inherent conflict in goals any alignment would mean one organization would inevitably drown the other. Given the current state of politics in America the sure loser will be the democratic one. However, when separate, they can complement each other.

33 Some groups may want to elect more formal representatives as recognized leaders. Such a step, if it is ever deemed necessary for a democratic group of this size, should be delayed until the fledgling organization has tackled a few projects and gotten its feet on the ground. Until the majority-based process has become habitual formal leadership will serve to concentrate authority in a few select hands. Given the small size of a block organization there is generally little need to grant such extensive authority to particular individuals.

34 An example of gaining coerced consent via intimidation ('if you don't fix your house, we will tell your new neighbors how you're treating your old ones') and harassment (having to repeatedly explain himself to his newly curious neighbors).

35 Koch, p. 604

36 American Heritage Dictionary of the English Language.

37 see the Afterward for a description of, and response to Putnam's work.

38 Wood, p. 58

39 ibid., p. 69.

40 ibid., p. 61.

41 Edward O. Wilson, *Consilience: The Unity of Knowledge* (New York: Alfred A. Knopf, 1998) p. 127-8.

42 Wilson, p. 127-8. "Culture is created by the communal mind, and each mind in turn is the product of the genetically structured human brain. Genes and culture are therefore inextricably linked. Certain cultural norms . . . survive and reproduce better than competing norms."

43 Robert Sampson, Stephen W. Raudenbush, Felton Earls "Neighborhoods and Violent Crime: A Multilevel Study of Collective Efficacy" *Science*, August 15, 1997. pp. 918-22.

[44] Robert Putnam, *Bowling Alone: The Collapse and Revival of American Community* (New York: Simon & Schuster) p. 43.

[45] ibid, p. 283.

[46] Putnam, p.268 - 272.

[47] song by Crosby, Stills, Nash, & Young.

[48] Putnam, 404